Just Cause or Just Because?

Prosecution and Plea-Bargaining Resulting in Prison Sentences on Low-Level Drug Charges in California and Arizona

K. Jack Riley, Nancy Rodriguez, Greg Ridgeway, Dionne Barnes-Proby, Terry Fain, Nell Griffith Forge, Vincent Webb

With Linda J. Demaine

Prepared for the Robert Woods Johnson Foundation SAPRP

 INFRASTRUCTURE, SAFETY, AND ENVIRONMENT

The research described in this report was supported by a grant from the Substance Abuse Policy Research Program of the Robert Wood Johnson Foundation. RAND and Arizona State University conducted this research in partnership. The study was conducted within RAND Infrastructure, Safety, and Environment (ISE), a unit of the RAND Corporation.

Library of Congress Cataloging-in-Publication Data

Just cause or just because? : prosecution and plea-bargaining resulting in prison
   sentences on low-level drug charges in California and Arizona / K. Jack Riley ...
   [et al.] ; with Linda J. Demaine.
      p. cm.
      "MG-288."
      Includes bibliographical references.
      ISBN 0-8330-3778-1 (pbk. : alk. paper)
      1. Sentences (Criminal procedure)—Arizona. 2. Sentences (Criminal
   procedure)—California. 3. Drugs of abuse—Law and legislation—Arizona—
   Criminal provisions. 4. Drugs of abuse—Law and legislation—California—
   Criminal provisions. I. Riley, Kevin Jack, 1964–

   KF9685.Z95J87 2005
   345.791'0277—dc22

                                                          2005007587

The RAND Corporation is a nonprofit research organization providing objective analysis and effective solutions that address the challenges facing the public and private sectors around the world. RAND's publications do not necessarily reflect the opinions of its research clients and sponsors.

RAND® is a registered trademark.

Published 2005 by the RAND Corporation
1776 Main Street, P.O. Box 2138, Santa Monica, CA 90407-2138
1200 South Hayes Street, Arlington, VA 22202-5050
201 North Craig Street, Suite 202, Pittsburgh, PA 15213-1516
RAND URL: http://www.rand.org/
To order RAND documents or to obtain additional information, contact
Distribution Services: Telephone: (310) 451-7002;
Fax: (310) 451-6915; Email: order@rand.org

Preface

As average sentence lengths have increased and spending on prisons and incarceration has risen, many have begun to question whether we are punishing one segment of the criminal population—low-level drug offenders—too harshly. Indeed, some ballot initiatives, such as Proposition 36 in California and Proposition 200 in Arizona, succeeded in part because voters agreed with these perceptions. These trends beg the question of how many low-level drug offenders end up in prison and what course of events led them to receive a prison sentence. In this report, we examine the original arrest charge(s), filing charge(s), plea-bargaining processes, and criminal histories of offenders who ultimately ended up in California and Arizona prisons on low-level drug charges. Although many thousands of offenders receive *jail* sentences for low-level drug offenses, we examine only *prison* sentences in this report.

This research was supported by a grant from the Substance Abuse Policy Research Program (SAPRP) of the Robert Wood Johnson Foundation. The RAND Corporation and Arizona State University conducted the research in partnership. This book extends a line of research that RAND has been instrumental in developing. Other recent examples of RAND's work in sentencing include the following:

- Jonathan P. Caulkins, C. Peter Rydell, William Schwabe, and James R. Chiesa, *Mandatory Minimum Drug Sentences: Throwing Away the Key or the Taxpayers' Money?* MR-827-DPRC, 1997

- Peter W. Greenwood, Karyn E. Model, C. Peter Rydell, and James R. Chiesa, *Diverting Children from a Life of Crime: Measuring Costs and Benefits,* MR-699-1-UCB/RC/IF, 1998
- Lynn A. Karoly, Peter W. Greenwood, Susan S. Everingham, Jill Hoube, M. Rebecca Kilburn, C. Peter Rydell, Matthew R. Sanders, James R. Chiesa, *Investing in Our Children: What We Know and Don't Know About the Costs and Benefits of Early Childhood Interventions,* MR-898-TCWF, 1998.

Recent Arizona State University documents on sentencing include the following:

- N. Rodriguez, "Sequential Analysis Among Minority Criminal Offenders: The Road to Becoming a Persistent Violent Offender," *Corrections Management Quarterly,* 4(1), 2000, 28–35
- N. Rodriguez, "The Impact Of 'Strikes' in Sentencing Decisions: Punishment for Only Some Habitual Offenders," *Criminal Justice Policy Review,* 14(1), 2003, 106–127.

This study was conducted within the Drug Policy Research Center (DPRC), a joint endeavor of the Safety and Justice Program of RAND Infrastructure, Safety and Environment (ISE) and RAND Health. RAND ISE and RAND Health are both divisions of the RAND Corporation. RAND ISE's mission is to improve the development, operation, use, and protection of society's essential built and natural assets and to enhance the safety and security of individuals in transit and in their workplaces and communities. The Safety and Justice Program addresses criminal justice issues, including sentencing and corrections policy, firearms, community violence, and drug policy. Inquiries regarding the mission of the DPRC may be directed to:

Peter Reuter
Co-Director, DPRC
RAND ISE
1200 South Hayes Street
Arlington, VA 22202
703-413-1100

Contents

Figures

Tables

Summary

Introduction

In 2000 and 1996, respectively, California and Arizona voters approved ballot initiatives that altered the prosecution of certain drug offenders and sought to make treatment more widely available. The voters were motivated by a mix of factors, including the perceived expense of incarceration, a desire to ensure imprisonment of violent offenders, the perceived harshness of drug sentences for low-level, particularly marijuana, offenders, and the lack of treatment availability for drug users. According to the California Legislative Analyst's Office, under Proposition 36 "an offender convicted of a 'nonviolent drug possession offense' would generally be sentenced to probation, instead of state prison, county jail, or probation without drug treatment."[1] In Arizona, the Drug Medicalization, Prevention and Control Act of 1996 (Proposition 200) established mandatory drug treatment for individuals convicted of possession or use of a controlled substance. Generally, both reforms were expected to divert minor, nonviolent drug offenders from incarceration (both jail and prison) to treatment. Although jailing of low-level drug offenders remains a major national issue, we focus here on offenders sentenced to

---

[1] California Legislative Analyst's Office, review of Proposition 36, http://www. lao.ca.gov/ballot/2000/36_11_2000.html, accessed on March 8, 2005.

prison for two reasons. First, the reform in California was expected to save far more resources ($200 million to $250 million) in prison costs than in jail costs ($40 million).[2] Second, the consequences of a prison sentence are often more severe than the consequences of a jail sentence, as measured by impact on family, employment prospects, and other social functioning indicators.

Although the initiatives passed overwhelmingly in both states, little was known about drug offenders who received prison sentences other than their increasingly large share of the prison population. Prosecutors asserted that they were already treating such drug offenders fairly by making appropriate referrals to treatment and substantial use of plea-bargains. Prosecutors' patterns had not been carefully examined, so it was unknown whether low-level drug offenders in prison had a violent or lengthy criminal history that made prosecutors reluctant to drop the low-level drug charge, whether the quantity or type of drug involved influenced the prosecution pattern, and whether there were differences across racial groups in the prosecution of low-level drug offenders.

This study set out to fill in gaps in our knowledge about the prosecution of imprisoned low-level drug offenders and how such prosecutions might be affected by diversion reform initiatives. It was designed to assess what proportion of offenders had merely "smoked a joint" (that is, their true underlying drug crime was minor) and had no or minimal prior record (that is, they were first-time offenders) versus the proportion who had been charged with a more severe crime and engaged in plea-bargaining or who had a severe criminal record. Answering these questions is important because the ballot initiatives were generally intended to divert the former category of offender from the prison track, and the anticipated savings were expected to come from these diversions. To accomplish the aims of the study, we do the following:

---

[2] California Legislative Analyst's Office, review of Proposition 36.

- *Characterize the prosecution of drug possession and other low-level offenses relative to drug sales and other nonpossession offenses.* For example, do such offenders have extensive criminal histories?
- *Examine how marijuana is treated relative to other drugs.* Are marijuana cases being prosecuted "too harshly," as some have argued?
- *Examine whether plea-bargaining practices are influenced by race.* If so, are certain racial groups are more likely than others to receive more lenient or severe treatment by prosecutors?
- *Examine what factors influence plea-bargaining behavior and plea-bargaining outcomes.* Plea-bargaining is the standard and widely accepted process under which both prosecutors and offenders negotiate, typically to effect sentencing on a lesser offense relative to the offender's initial arrest and filing charges. In accepting the plea-bargain, both sides forgo the uncertainty of a trial outcome—the prosecutor obtains a sure conviction and the offender avoids the possibility of a lengthier prison sentence.
- *Analyze whether Proposition 200 has brought about changes in drug prosecution patterns,* given Arizona's longer experience with a reform initiative.

Study Design and Methodology

The definition of low-level drug offense for the California portion of the study was drawn from the language of Proposition 36 and modified to correct for, or incorporate, ambiguities, errors, and omissions. In Arizona, similar methodology was applied, resulting in a definition of "low level" that included drug possession, drug use, and paraphernalia offenses.

In California, the research team drew a sample from the more than 23,000 offenders imprisoned on low-level drug offenses from specified urban counties in 1998 and 1999, the last years of sentencing activities prior to the emergence of the Proposition 36 campaign in California. In Arizona, data were available electronically for the 4,931 low-level drug commitments that occurred between 1996 and

2000. This four-year span includes a period prior to and after implementation of Proposition 200.

For both California and Arizona, the researchers developed an offense severity index for past arrests and convictions, a criminal history index, and a measure of the plea-bargaining that occurred in the offender's case. The plea-bargaining measure was defined as the distance along the severity index between arrest charges and charges at conviction. The team also collected data on sociodemographic characteristics that might have influenced prosecution, including race, age, gender, employment status, and county. The type of drug was obtained from the prosecution records. In California, the quantity of drug could be obtained from records, but in Arizona the team had to utilize more general quantity measurements (for instance, "baggies" or "rocks").

Drug Prosecutions Resulting in Prison Terms in the Pre-Proposition Eras

Imprisoned Low-Level Drug Offenders in California

The California population consisted primarily of males who were unemployed at the time of their offense. Approximately one-third were black, one-third were Latinos, and almost one-third were white. Nearly 30 percent were on probation at the time of their offense. Almost 50 percent of the cases involved cocaine and fewer than 3 percent involved marijuana only. Approximately 7 percent originated at arrest as drug transportation or sale cases. Offenders had an average of 9.8 prior arrests and 3.9 prior convictions (with a sum severity score[3] of 195 for prior offenses) in their record. Low-level drug offenders had an average of 3.4 charges filed by prosecutors and had received sentences averaging 29.4 months.

---

[3] Each previous conviction offense is given a score from 1 (low severity) to 74 (high severity). The sum severity score for an individual is the total of these scores for each previous conviction. For the California sample, the offenders averaged 3.9 previous convictions with a sum severity score of 195. Thus, each of the 3.9 previous convictions had an average severity score of 50, which represents a relatively severe felony.

Key research findings include the following:

- Sixty-eight percent of those in prison on a drug sales charge had a previous drug conviction (78 percent had a previous conviction of some sort); 72 percent of those in prison on a non-sales charge had a previous drug conviction (98 percent had a previous conviction of some sort).
- Plea-bargaining from a drug sales charge to a non-sales charge was relatively rare: Only 11 percent of those convicted on non-sales charges had originally been charged with a drug sale or transport offense. This pattern did not differ across drugs, including marijuana.
- Cases involving large amounts of drugs (200 grams and over) were likely to start out and remain sales cases; instances involving smaller amounts either originated as sales cases but were disposed of as non-sales cases or originated and ended as non-sales cases. The median marijuana offender had 246 grams at arrest and the median cocaine offender had 46 grams at arrest.
- Imprisoned non-sales offenders had more severe criminal histories than imprisoned sales offenders. This finding holds true even when type of drug and county of prosecution are controlled for. On average, however, cocaine offenders had roughly twice as many criminal convictions in their history as marijuana offenders.
- By drug type, 60 percent of imprisoned marijuana offenders had a previous drug conviction of one sort or another (79 percent had a prior conviction of some kind). In contrast, 70 percent of cocaine offenders had prior drug convictions (97 percent of them had prior convictions of some kind).
- Drug type, but not race, seemed to influence charge reductions, with marijuana offenses most frequently resulting in a reduction.

Imprisoned Low-Level Drug Offenders in Arizona

In Arizona, 81 percent of low-level drug offenders were male. The majority were white, followed by Latinos and blacks. Seventy percent were unemployed at arrest. Nearly 60 percent were probationers.

About 13 percent of all imprisoned low-level drug cases were for marijuana, about 25 percent for dangerous drugs, about 33 percent for narcotic drugs, and about 25 percent for paraphernalia. Prior to Proposition 200, offenders had an average of 8.32 prior arrests and 17.1 prior offenses in their record (with a sum severity score of 671.5 for prior offenses).[4] On average, low-level drug offenders in the weighted sample were sentenced to prison for 1.9 years pre-Proposition 200.

Key findings include the following:

- Drug quantities were not consistently and accurately recorded as part of the case files, but narratives from police arrest records indicate that the overwhelming majority of sale, transportation, and importation offenses appeared to involve large quantities.
- Most case adjustments took place from the time of arrest to prosecution. Offenders with more extensive and serious prior records were more likely to have the charges reduced. Conversely, the less extensive the prior record, the more likely offenders were to have charges added from arrest to prosecution.
- Between arrest and prosecution, marijuana offenders were less likely than other drug offenders to have a change in charges or in sum severity score.
- The number of charges from arrest to prosecution decreased for a larger percentage of Latinos convicted on marijuana and dangerous drug offenses than for whites and blacks. Charges were reduced for fewer blacks convicted of narcotic drug offenses than for other ethnic groups. White offenders experienced the most case adjustments.
- For probationers, most plea-bargaining activity took place from the time of the probation revocation to prosecution. Charges were more likely to decrease for probationers with the fewest and least severe criminal records. Conversely, charges were more

---

[4] A single arrest can include multiple offenses.

likely to increase for probationers with more extensive and severe criminal records.

Factors Influencing Plea-Bargaining

California prosecutors first file the arrest charges and may also file additional charges and enhancements before plea-bargaining begins. Thus, negotiated reductions in charges occur between the filing of charges and sentencing. In Arizona, on the other hand, plea-bargaining occurs between the arrest and the filing of charges.

In California, age, drug type, county, and the number of charges filed were significantly associated with patterns in reduction of charges. Surprisingly, the number of prior convictions was not a significant factor in the likelihood of experiencing charge reductions.

In Arizona, charge severity scores tended to decrease more for males than for females, and charges were more likely to be decreased for employed offenders than for unemployed offenders. Higher rates of plea-bargaining or case adjustments were more likely in dangerous drug and paraphernalia cases than in marijuana cases. Cases with a drug sale charge at arrest were more likely to involve a charge severity score decrease; charge severity scores tended to decrease as the number of counts increased. Charge severity scores for offenders with more extensive prior records were more likely to decrease than to remain the same.

Summary and Policy Implications

Severity. The evidence supports the hypotheses of prosecutors that, prior to the implementation of Proposition 36 and Proposition 200, offenders convicted on low-level drug charges generally had more severe criminal histories, were involved with harder drugs (cocaine, heroin), or were caught with substantial quantities. The findings support prosecutors' contention that low-level offenders receiving prison sentences had more serious and extensive criminal histories than the "low-level" conviction label suggests.

In California, people imprisoned on non-sales charges (primarily possession) had more severe criminal histories than those imprisoned on sales charges, suggesting that criminal history is an aggravating factor that helps equalize the severity of sales and non-sales offenses in the eyes of the law. In Arizona, low-level offenders were arrested with relatively large quantities of drugs and allowed to plead down to low-level offenses, distorting the true nature of low-level drug offenders in prison.

Marijuana Offenders. The treatment of marijuana offenders is less clear. In California, the small number of marijuana offenders generally had less severe criminal histories (as measured by the number of arrests and convictions and the severity score of arrest charges and convictions) but larger quantities of drugs. Thus, quantity may be playing a role in increasing the severity with which marijuana offenders are being treated.

Although there were proportionately few marijuana offenders in Arizona, marijuana cases were also characterized by offenders' extensive and severe criminal history records. Arizona marijuana offenders averaged 10 prior arrests and 17 prior offenses. A qualitative review of drug quantities shows that a substantial percentage (about 17 percent) of Arizona's low-level drug offenders were originally arrested for offenses that included sales, transportation, and importation of drugs. These findings depict an imprisoned population with far more severe drug offenses than the one portrayed in prior studies. Taken together, they serve as evidence that marijuana offenders are not first- or second-time offenders and are not treated more "harshly" or more "leniently" than other drug offenders.

Race/Ethnicity. A bivariate analysis of pre–Proposition 200 data in Arizona shows that race and ethnicity played a role in charging decisions, with whites having more case adjustments than blacks or Latinos. However, once multivariate analyses were conducted, the race effects disappeared and there were no racial/ethnic disparities in plea outcomes prior to Proposition 200. Gender, employment status, and legal criteria (e.g., drug sales, paraphernalia cases, dangerous drugs, and prior record) were the significant predictors of plea outcomes.

Did Prosecution Patterns Change After Ballot Reform in Arizona?

At the time the research was funded, a before-and-after examination of the initiative's effects was possible only in Arizona. In Arizona, we examined the following questions: (1) Were offenders' prior records more severe and lengthy after enactment of the proposition? (2) What was the overall prevalence of plea-bargaining? (3) Did sale and paraphernalia charges have a direct influence on plea outcomes post–Proposition 200? Concerning the first question, we would expect a reduction in the overall severity of offense indices for incarcerated offenders because Proposition 200 excludes violent offenders. The second question addresses whether offenders no longer see treatment as an incentive to plead and are now less willing to accept a plea to dispose their cases. The third question was examined to see if sale charges increased and produced more severe plea outcomes. We also tested whether paraphernalia charges increased post–proposition 200 as a new mechanism to encourage plea-bargain opportunities.

Findings
After Proposition 200, the proportion of females and blacks and the proportion of paraphernalia cases in the imprisoned population increased, whereas the proportion of marijuana and probation offenders decreased. Key analytic findings include the following:

- Except for paraphernalia cases, charges were more likely to decrease in the post–Proposition 200 environment, regardless of drug type.
- Post-proposition data show that offenders' prior records were more extensive and severe in nature and less varied across the range of severity scores. In the plea-bargaining phase, severity scores were more likely to decrease pre–Proposition 200.
- Although it is difficult to assess whether prosecution patterns changed by race after implementation of Proposition 200, the data do indicate that Latinos were treated more severely than

other racial/ethnic groups, a finding that must be caveated by the small number of cases for this comparison.

Policy Implications

Prosecution and sentencing patterns changed in Arizona after passage of Proposition 200. Offenders incarcerated after Proposition 200 had more extensive and severe criminal records. Evidence of post-Proposition 200 "hardening" in the processing of low-level drug offenders is reflected in the finding that the proportion of prosecuted and imprisoned drug cases involving paraphernalia cases increased after Proposition 200. The uncertainty regarding how paraphernalia cases should be processed—at least until Arizona's Supreme Court decides the issue—may be the reason for such an increase. (Some jurisdictions treated paraphernalia cases as eligible for treatment under the new law; others excluded them altogether.)

Our data analysis reveals that, after Proposition 200, the more extensive an arrestee's criminal history, the more severe the charges were likely to be. Thus, a prior record may now serve to enhance rather than reduce punishment (the latter was the case prior to the implementation of the proposition). Interestingly, the proportion of marijuana offenders not only decreased after implementation but those offenders were also far less likely to have an increase in severity from arrest to sentencing. Post-proposition prosecutorial decision-making processes appear to be characterized by decreased severity for marijuana cases, increased severity for paraphernalia cases, and increased severity for cases with extensive prior records.

Some have argued that the marked increase in the prosecution and incarceration of paraphernalia offenders after Proposition 200 was a way to circumvent the intent of the proposition. However, incarcerated paraphernalia offenders share many of the same characteristics of other low-level drug offenders—they have extensive criminal histories. In sum, it does not appear that new prosecution practices after Proposition 200 had the effect of blocking the diversion to treatment of drug offenders or resulted in the incarceration of large numbers of nonserious offenders.

Lessons from California and Arizona

This study set out to fill in gaps in our knowledge about the prosecution of imprisoned low-level drug offenders. What are the characteristics of low-level drug offenders who end up in prison? What is the role of plea-bargaining and what factors affect it? Do outcomes vary systematically by race and ethnicity? Finally, what effect did passage of Proposition 200 in Arizona in 1996 have on drug prosecution and imprisonment?

Plea-bargaining for drug offenses that result in prison sentences appears to be used in a manner consistent with prosecutorial practices aimed at incarcerating drug offenders who are perceived to present a greater threat to the community due to criminal involvement or involvement in more serious forms of drug offenses. In our samples, the low-level drug offenders in prison are often much more serious offenders than the "low-level" label implies. Indeed, imprisoned low-level drug offenders tend to have criminal histories reflecting their involvement in a variety of criminal offenses, cases involving large quantities of drugs, or both.

Additionally, given that the pathway to incarceration for the majority of Arizona's low-level drug offenders is probation, there is a need for additional research to examine the decisionmaking practices that lead to probation revocation and incarceration. Research will need to go beyond the prosecution function and examine the role of probation officials in making those decisions as well as the decisionmaking processes that lead to chain of events culminating in the incarceration of low-level drug offenders.

Acknowledgments

Jeff Rubin from the Alameda County District Attorney's office was an invaluable source of support on this project. He tirelessly cajoled his counterparts in other jurisdictions to participate and provided the project staff with many valuable insights about abstracting data from prosecution files. Our project would have been diminished in quality and comprehensiveness without his contributions.

We would also like to thank Larry Brown, former Executive Director of the California District Attorney's Association (CDAA). Larry was instrumental in securing access to prosecution files in the sample counties. He was a key contributor to the completion of this project.

We thank Vicki Sands of the California Department of Justice who acquired California Department of Justice data for us and responded to our detailed questions.

We thank the former Maricopa County Attorney, Rick M. Romley, and Executive Chief, Carol MacFadden, for their guidance throughout this project. The County Attorney's Office provided much direction on prosecution policy and data collection and was instrumental in soliciting the cooperation of other agencies. We appreciate the support received from Dr. Elizabeth Eells from the Arizona Supreme Court, Administrative Office of the Courts, who was an invaluable resource throughout the research process. We thank Dr. Darrell Fischer, Data Manager of the Arizona Department of Corrections, who provided us with population data on low-level drug offenders in Arizona. To all the staff of the Arizona Department of

Corrections, especially Donna Clement, Lydia Johnson, Freda Harris, and Roberta Alcover, who worked diligently on retrieving offenders' case files, we are grateful for your efforts. We thank the Arizona Department of Public Safety, in particular Patty Morris and John Halka who provided access to criminal history records of offenders in Arizona. Many thanks to Melanie K. Fay and J. Ed Morris of the Maricopa County Clerk of Superior Court who accommodated data collectors and worked on the retrieval of case files for offenders sentenced in Maricopa County.

Pamela K. Lattimore and Doug Longshore conducted an independent review of our report. They are, respectively, national experts on sentencing and drug policy issues. Our manuscript is stronger because of their efforts. In addition, RAND colleagues Peter Reuter, Andrew Morral, and Susan Turner provided important critical inputs and our editor, Miriam Polon, helped shape the document substantially. We are grateful for their efforts.

Last, we appreciate all the time and effort of the data abstractors who worked with the respective agencies to collect the data: Sylvia Coleman, Elizabeth Doroski, Rhonda Lewis, Edward T. Lin, Kristin Nakashima, and Patricia Nwajuaku all worked diligently to ensure that we had accurate and comprehensive data. We'd also like to thank Stella Bart for entering the data as well.

Though indebted to the many who assisted on this project, the authors remain solely responsible for any errors and omissions.

Acronyms

AG	attorney general
AZDOC	Arizona Department of Corrections
CDAA	California District Attorneys Association
CDC	California Department of Corrections
DA	district attorney
DEA	Drug Enforcement Administration
ESS	effective sample size
FY	fiscal year
LAO	Legislative Analyst's Office (California)
MJ	marijuana
ONDCP	Office of National Drug Control Policy
SES	socioeconomic status

CHAPTER ONE

Introduction

In 2000 and 1996, respectively, California and Arizona voters approved ballot initiatives with the potential to have far-reaching effects on how the criminal justice system handles drug offenders. The passage of these initiatives was largely motivated by a growing belief among both advocacy organizations and voters that there is something wrong with drug sentencing. Examples of the "wrongs" claimed include the expense of incarcerating drug offenders relative to violent criminals, the harshness (length, certainty, etc.) of drug sentencing, and the harshness with which marijuana offenses were treated. There were concerns that too many first-time drug offenders were going to jail and prison for possession or other low-level offenses. Advocates of the types of reforms embodied in propositions 36 and 200 expect that the diversion of minor, nonviolent drug offenders from incarceration to treatment will reap benefits in the form of reduced criminality and reduced substance abuse. Opponents of these reforms typically point to the countervailing argument: Offenders with criminal tendencies bypass incarceration and are put on the streets where they can commit additional crimes.

The objective of this report is not to examine the fundamental question of whether diversion to treatment reduces criminality or substance abuse or places criminals on the streets, nor even to assess the efficacy or effect of the reform initiatives. Rather, the objective is to examine the course by which offenders ended up in *prison* on low-level drug charges in California and Arizona, two states that sought through ballot initiatives to reduce the severity with which drug offenders are treated. The jailing, as opposed to imprisonment, of low-level drug offenders is an important issue, but one that is not addressed in this document. We focus on imprisoned offenders both because of the higher anticipated savings ($200 million to $250 million for prisoners, according to the California Legislative Analyst's Office [LAO], as opposed to $40 million for jails) and because the consequences of imprisonment (loss of voting privileges, family disruption, reduced employment prospects) tend to be more severe than for jail.[1]

Do such prisoners have severe criminal histories? In cases that are alike except for the drug involved, do marijuana offenders have more or less severe criminal histories than other drug offenders? In conducting this examination, we highlight a stage of the criminal justice system—prosecution—that rarely receives scrutiny. In particular, we examine whether plea-bargaining practices facilitate or hinder the processing of imprisoned low-level drug offenders in these two states.

This study has five objectives:

- To characterize the prosecution resulting in prison sentences of drug possession offenses relative to drug sales and other nonpossession offenses.
- To examine how marijuana is treated relative to other drugs.
- To explore the racial implications of drug sentencing and plea-bargaining practices.
- To examine what factors influence plea-bargaining behavior and plea-bargaining outcomes.
- To analyze whether Arizona's Proposition 200 has brought about changes in drug prosecution patterns that result in prison sentences.

---

[1] Cost savings estimates are found at California Legislative Analyst's Office, review of Proposition 36, accessed at http://www.lao.ca.gov/ballot/2000/36_11_2000.html on March 8, 2005.

Trends in Drug Sentencing

Over the course of the past two decades, two ineluctable facts about the U.S. criminal justice system have emerged. Perhaps most obviously, drug offenders constitute an increasingly large portion of the prison population, according to the Bureau of Justice Statistics (BJS) (2000). Drug offenders constituted 21 percent of all sentenced state inmates in 1998 and accounted for 19 percent of the total growth in state inmates from 1990 to 1998. Perhaps less obviously, drug offenders are, with greater certainty, serving longer sentences behind bars. These patterns occur in an environment where a small percentage of criminal offenses go to trial and a large percentage of offenses are settled through some form of negotiation, that is, in an environment where plea-bargains are common (Forst, 1995; Tonry and Coffee, 1992).

A number of factors helped form these sentencing patterns. In 1986 the federal government enacted a substantial shift in drug sentencing that was intended to focus on drug trafficking and distribution (United States Sentencing Commission, 1995). The new federal sentencing policy was linked to the drug quantities—measured in total weight, including adulterants—involved in the transaction. Convictions involving drug quantities at or above certain threshold weights triggered sentences of predetermined length (the mandatory portion), of which a specified amount of time had to be served before the individual could be released (the minimum portion). These sentences can be applied to defendants who are convicted *solely* of drug possession and who have *no other criminal history*. Many states later modified their sentencing statutes based on the federal model. For example, although New York had strict drug sentencing laws dating back as far as 1973, the state lowered the weight thresholds for cocaine and crack in 1988, a move that resulted in even stricter sentences. By 1995, 14 states distinguished between crack and powder cocaine; 21 had enacted sentencing guideline systems; and 32 had some form of mandatory minimums (United States Sentencing Commission, 1995), California and Arizona among them. Although the sentences are mandatory and linked to quantitative thresholds, some also contain a safety valve that prevents the sentences from being imposed unless the court is satisfied that the offender was substantially involved in planning, directing, executing, or financing the underlying offense. The language is intended to provide relief for offenders who, for example, unknowingly transported large quantities of drugs.[2]

The Push for Reform

The rigidity of the drug sentencing structures that emerged in the 1980s and 1990s has spawned much criticism and, lately, the formation of advocacy groups leading efforts at reform.[3] Advocacy organizations have noted that mandatory sentencing provides multiple opportunities for inequities, including the potential for racial disparity in sentencing outcomes; disproportionate disenfranchisement of minorities from voting privileges; variations in sentencing by drug type; and the severity of drug sentences relative to crimes with direct victims (Human Rights Watch, 1997; Norris, Conrad, and Resner, 1998; Sentencing Project, 1998).

The rigidity of mandatory minimum sentences, the concerns about racial disparity in drug prosecutions, and the concerns about the treatment of marijuana offenders have stirred public concern and spurred the development of organized efforts to address these policy issues. In California and Arizona, residents approved ballot initiatives with potentially far-reaching consequences for drug sentencing. In both cases, the initiatives were sponsored by organized individuals and groups intent on achieving drug reform.[4]

---

[2] For more on safety valves and a review of the federal safety valve, see Bernstein (1995).

[3] See for example the Campaign for Treatment Not Jail, at www.treatnotjail.org, and Families Against Mandatory Minimums, at www.famm.org.

[4] In Arizona, the initiative was sponsored by The People Have Spoken (formerly Arizonans for Drug Policy Reform) and funded by George Soros, Peter Lewis, and John Sperling.

California and Proposition 36

Prior to the October 2000 election, the California Legislative Analyst's Office developed a short definition of Proposition 36:

> Under this proposition . . . an offender convicted of a "nonviolent drug possession offense" would generally be sentenced to probation, instead of state prison, county jail, or probation without drug treatment.[5]

The initiative passed overwhelmingly—61 percent to 39 percent and represented in part, a backlash to California's Three Strikes sentencing program. Effectively, Proposition 36 is a post-conviction program that diverts eligible offenders from prisons, jails, and nontreatment probation sentences to probation with terms of treatment. Proposition 36 directly addresses simple drug possession and drug use offenses. There are other offenses that the initiative's language appeared to incorporate, at least in part, or that did not exist under California penal codes. For example, the language of the proposition described an offense—transportation of a controlled substance for personal use—that did not exist in statute law. Offenders previously convicted of violent or serious crimes, individuals concurrently convicted of a felony other than a nonviolent drug possession offense, and individuals concurrently convicted of a misdemeanor not related to the use of drugs are ineligible for Proposition 36.

Arizona and Proposition 200

In Arizona, the Drug Medicalization, Prevention and Control Act of 1996 (Proposition 200) established mandatory drug treatment for individuals convicted of possession or use of a controlled substance. Shortly after its passage, the Arizona legislature repealed the act and proposed propositions to limit those defendants who would be eligible for mandatory treatment. The sponsors of Proposition 200 countered such actions with an initiative to reject the legislature's proposed changes. During the 1998 election, the voters rejected the

---

[5] California Legislative Analyst's Office, review of Proposition 36.

legislature's proposed changes and the original terms of the act were once again in force.

Although Proposition 200 was intended to provide treatment for drug offenders, paraphernalia cases were not specifically addressed in the act. Given no clear indication on how paraphernalia cases should be processed, jurisdictions handled such cases in varying ways. Some jurisdictions regarded paraphernalia cases alone as eligible for treatment or eligible only when they involved possession or use of controlled substances; others excluded paraphernalia cases altogether from the treatment eligible provisions. These different interpretations regarding the applicability of mandatory drug treatment in paraphernalia cases led to two divergent decisions from Division I and Division II of the Arizona Court of Appeals. In 2001, the Arizona Supreme Court ruled that mandatory drug treatment applies to paraphernalia cases "where the presence of paraphernalia is associated only with personal use by individuals simultaneously charged, or who could have been simultaneously charged, with possession or use under 13-901.01."[6] Although some paraphernalia cases were included in the Proposition 200 provision, the Arizona Department of Corrections (AZDOC) reported an increase in the commitment of paraphernalia offenders after the enactment of Proposition 200.

The California and Arizona initiatives address two particular aspects of drug sentencing. Perhaps most importantly, they address the issue that drug sentencing is "too harsh." The initiatives address the issue of sentencing harshness by generally making possession and other low-level offenders with nonviolent records eligible for diversion from prison to community-based treatment. In addition, the initiatives implicitly seek to distinguish marijuana offenses from other drug offenses, since marijuana offenses tend to cluster at the less-severe end of criminal codes and since marijuana offenders are believed to be less likely to have a violent criminal history.

---

[6] *State v. Estrada,* 201 Ariz. 247, 34 P.3d 356 (2001).

The Prosecution of Offenders Under Drug Sentencing Reforms

Most prosecutors would assert that they treat drug offenders fairly and that the ballot reforms are misguided efforts that limit their ability to make appropriate bargains with offenders during prosecution (see, for example, Orloff, 2000). California's 1994 Three Strikes initiative, which was motivated by a violent crime committed by a paroled felon, is one example of how the criminal justice system, particularly prosecutions, can re-equilibrate in response to a new law. Initially, judges were explicitly prohibited from removing prior convictions for serious felonies from the "strike" count, although court challenges later restored that capability. The Three Strikes law allowed prosecutors to waive prior strikes if they would have trouble proving them or "in the furtherance of justice." Discretion was thus transferred from judges to prosecutors.

Lessons from Prosecution Research

The push for drug sentencing reform occurs in the absence of solid empirical information about key aspects of drug prosecutions. Most analyses of drug sentencing trends are limited by the lack of data on the prosecution process—more specifically, the plea-bargaining—that occurs during prosecution. Human Rights Watch (Human Rights Watch, 1997) examined New York state drug sentencing patterns and concluded that more than 80 percent of those imprisoned in 1997 had no prior violent convictions, more than 50 percent had no prior violent arrests, and nearly 32 percent were first-time felony offenders. In addition, Human Rights Watch found that 63 percent were convicted on class C, D, and E felonies—the lowest felony class levels. A study of all state drug offenders also found that 21 percent of offenders were first-time offenders, 43 percent were convicted of drug possession, and 71 percent reported no involvement in activities that could constitute "high-level" drug activities.

This work, while important, has two limitations from the perspective of this project. First, it does not examine plea-bargaining strategies, so we cannot determine what portion of offenders convicted in the lowest felony classes pled down from higher felony classes. Thus, we cannot determine the extent to which plea behavior is a function of criminal history, the quantity of the drug involved at arrest, and so forth. Second, the work does not break down sentence outcomes by drug type. Thus, it is impossible to determine from the studies whether the violent crime history is constant across drug types or whether those with nonviolent histories are disproportionately concentrated in drugs such as marijuana.

A recent study based on data from the Survey of Inmates in Federal and State Correctional Facilities addressed some of these limitations by defining low-level drug offenders and measuring their presence in prisons (Sevigny and Caulkins, 2004). This analysis reveals that most drug offenders were involved neither in mere drug use *nor* in drug trafficking with an organizational role. In fact, offenders who were nonviolent and had no sophisticated role in the drug offense and no other drug convictions accounted for 27 percent of federal and 23 percent of state drug prisoners. Findings on the role of drug quantity reveal that more than 50 percent of prisoners in state facilities and more than 90 percent of federal prisoners were sentenced in cases that involved more than ten retail units of drugs. These offenders were also first or second time drug-only offenders, were involved in nonviolent/nongun offenses, and had a minor role in drug distribution. Interestingly, a very small proportion of all drug inmates (less than 1 percent) were nonviolent, had possessed a small quantity of marijuana, and were not involved in drug distribution. The authors conclude that most offenders in prison can be classified as "ambiguous middle of the spectrum" drug offenders (p. 425).

Among those sentencing studies that have highlighted the role of plea-bargaining, several relationships have been substantiated. First, pleading guilty directly influences the sentencing outcomes of drug defendants. In particular, pleading guilty significantly reduces sentence severity (Albonetti, 1997; Hagan, 1981; Miethe, 1987; Rhodes, 1991; Ulmer and Kramer, 1996). However, studies have found that plea-bargaining practices may, in fact, produce racial disparity in sentencing practices (Berlin, 1993; Nagel, 1990; Reitz, 1993; Rhodes, 1991; Roberts, 1994; Schulhofer, 1992; Standen,

1993; Tonry, 1996; Yellen, 1993). Second, plea-bargaining serves to mediate the role of offender and case-specific factors (Standen, 1993). For example, Zatz (1984) found that pleading guilty resulted in more severe sentences for Latinos than for whites and lengthier sentences for Latinos than black defendants. However, Moore and Miethe (1986) found that under Minnesota's sentencing guidelines, guilty pleas did not produce any racial disparity. Similarly, Albonetti's (1997) study of federal offenders revealed that the effect of pleading guilty did not vary across racial groups. Most recently, Kautt and Spohn (2002) report that among federal drug offenders, going to trial has a greater *aggravating* effect for blacks than for whites under mandatory minimums. However, they also find that drug type (crack and heroin) and drug quantity (crack) serve to *mitigate* the sentences of black defendants versus white defendants.

Although most research on determinate sentencing systems has placed a minimal analytical focus on prosecutorial discretion, a few studies have examined the relationship of charging and plea-bargaining practices. Miethe and Moore examined prosecutorial discretion in charging and plea-bargaining decisions in Minnesota before and after the introduction of guidelines and found that such practices varied over time. Their study is limited in that different types of charge bargaining measures were combined to produce one measure of bargaining. Miethe (1987) addressed this limitation in a subsequent study and found no proof of prosecutorial "overcharging" during the post-guideline periods to encourage defendants to plead guilty to a reduced charge. In fact, the average severity of initial charge decreased during the post-guideline period. Although pre-guideline models of charge dismissal, charge reductions, and sentence concessions were significantly different across time periods, differences in the models were primarily attributed to case- and offense-specific attributes.

Unanswered Questions

Although there is a push for reform, there is very little empirical analysis or benchmarking against which to judge reforms, such as Proposition 36 and Proposition 200, that have the potential to fundamentally alter the prosecution of drug offenses. This report, then, seeks to address five specific gaps in our understanding of how imprisoned low-level drug offenses are prosecuted and how the reform manifested in Propositions 36 and 200 might change such prosecution. First, we seek to characterize the prosecution of cases that result in a prison sentence on a low-level drug charge. For example, do such offenders have extensive criminal histories? Second, we seek to examine how marijuana is treated relative to other drugs among cases that result in a prison sentence on a low-level drug charge. That is, we seek to examine whether marijuana cases are being prosecuted "too harshly." Third, we seek to explore the racial implications of drug sentencing and plea-bargaining practices. The objective here is to examine what kinds of racial disparities, if any, exist in the prosecution and imprisonment of such cases. Fourth, we explore the role of plea-bargaining generally in the drug prosecution context. That is, we examine what factors influence plea-bargaining behavior and plea-bargaining outcomes. Fifth, we use Arizona, which now has several years of post-proposition data available, to analyze whether Proposition 200 has brought about changes in drug prosecution patterns. (Such analysis was not possible for California at the time this research was conducted.) Each of these gaps is explored in greater depth in the subsections below.

The Prosecution and Imprisonment of Low-Level Drug Offenders

From a prosecution perspective, it is misleading to look at the number of people in prison on low-level charges and make inferences about sentence severity. Prosecutors argue that if an individual ends up in prison on a drug possession charge it is because of one of the following circumstances:

- The offender had a violent or lengthy criminal history that made prosecutors reluctant to drop the low-level drug charge.
- The offender had a less severe or violent criminal history, but was caught with a substantial amount of drugs and was allowed to plead down from a sales offense to a possession offense (Riley, et al., 2000).

Prosecutors (and other court officials) argue that drug offenders who are eligible and appropriate candidates for treatment would certainly be afforded such treatment even in the absence of the propositions. Further, some officials (e.g., the former Maricopa County Attorney) have argued that offenders often end up in prison because they fail treatment attempts or would rather go to prison in lieu of meeting community-based treatment requirements. Thus, in some important respects the sentencing of drug offenders in the criminal justice system is affected by offenders' willingness to receive treatment.

A review of California's prison commitments for drug possession shows a steady increase between 1980 and 1990 and again from 1992 to 1998 (see Figure 1.1). By 1998, more than 12,000 offenders were annually imprisoned on drug possession charges, and commitments for combined drug sales and manufacturing had risen steadily for years and then leveled off at approximately 11,000.[7]

Prosecutors contend that if a low-level drug offender, particularly a drug possessor, is imprisoned, it is because the offender had a violent or extensive criminal history or pled down to a lower offense because he was caught with a significant quantity of drugs. Many prosecutors interpret the growth in the population incarcerated for possession as evidence that they are successfully prosecuting drug sellers or offenders with serious criminal histories. These offenders, they

---

[7] These counts include new commitments, parole violations with new terms, and parole returns to custody. As discussed later, we consider only new commitments for our analysis. However, the data could not be broken down by commitment type for the years prior to 1997. Thus, Figure 1.1 presents aggregate commitment data.

Figure 1.1
Total California Prison Commitments of Drug Offenders

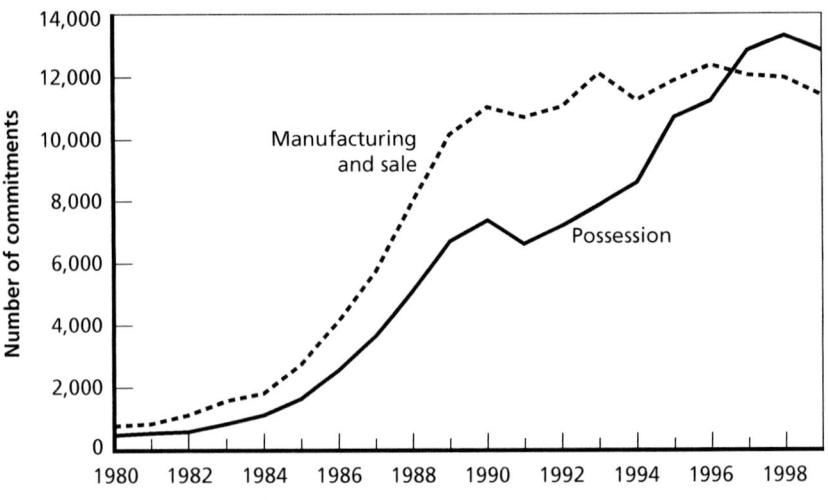

RAND MG288-1.1

argue, accept a drug possession prison sentence in lieu of more substantial penalties that might apply to their arrest charge or criminal history. Recent analysis conducted by the Alameda County (California) District Attorney supports the prosecutors' argument (Orloff, 2000). Orloff reports:

> [A]t least half of the individuals that went to state prison on straight drug possession charges went because they were allowed to plead to straight drug possession as a lesser included charge of a sale or possession for sale of drugs case. In some of these cases, other felony charges were dismissed in light of the plea to the straight drug possession case. . . . In other cases, individuals were on probation for straight possession but were sent to prison because they violated probation by selling drugs. . . . In the very few cases where the individuals went to state prison for a drug possession offense (i.e., not [pled down from] sales) . . . they are individuals with horrendous criminal records whom nobody . . . would want on the streets. Over 60 percent [of imprisoned drug possession offenders] were sent to state prison on [charges pled down from] sales cases,

or had other pending felonies dismissed or were sentenced on other felonies at the same time.

Similar outcomes were predicted in Arizona. For example, research conducted by the Maricopa County Attorney's Office called into question projected savings from Proposition 200 by noting that offenders convicted of drug possession had far more serious original charges and/or had lengthy criminal history records.[8] A key objective of this analysis is to examine whether the hypothesis offered by the prosecutors is correct.

Marijuana Offenses

According to FBI Uniform Crime Report statistics, more people were arrested on marijuana charges (nearly 700,000) in 1999 than were arrested on heroin and cocaine charges combined (528,000). We also know that, overall, sale and manufacturing offenses account for just less than 20 percent of drug arrests, of which about 9 percent are for heroin or cocaine and about 5 percent for marijuana. In contrast, about 80 percent of the national arrests involve drug possession, of which about 21 percent are for heroin or cocaine and nearly 40 percent are for marijuana. These statistics do not provide any information about the disposition of the cases. That is, we cannot tell what fraction went to jail versus prison, nor do we know anything about the relative sentence lengths. Nevertheless, the marijuana arrest figures are striking and at a minimum merit further examination to see if they support the prosecutors' contention that they seek prison terms for marijuana offenses only if they involve offenders with severe criminal histories or large quantities of drugs.

The Role of Race

Prior research has documented the relationship between race, plea-bargaining, and drug sentencing outcomes. While some studies show

---

[8] Errol J. Chavez, Special Agent in Charge, Drug Enforcement Administration, Phoenix Division, recently challenged claims that drug offenders are incarcerated for mere use of illegal drugs. He argued that offenders imprisoned for possession are there as a result of plea-bargains involving reduced or dropped charges.

a strong race effect, others show that the effect of race is either indirectly related to sentencing outcomes or not as strong a predictor as other measures (e.g., criminal history record). In this study, we examine whether plea-bargaining practices are influenced by race and, if so, whether certain racial groups are more likely than others to receive more lenient or severe treatment by prosecutors.

Plea-Bargaining Patterns

Plea-bargaining is the standard and widely accepted process under which both prosecutors and offenders negotiate, typically to effect sentencing on a lesser offense relative to the offender's initial arrest and filing charges. In accepting the plea-bargain, both sides forgo the uncertainty of a trial outcome—the prosecutor obtains a sure conviction and the offender avoids the possibility of a lengthier prison sentence. Plea-bargaining is the grease that makes the criminal justice system work. It is a highly discretionary practice: Both prosecutors and offenders must assess factors such as the strength of the case, the offender's prior record, the availability of resources, and other factors in deciding whether to entertain a plea. In the context of prosecuting low-level drug offenses, a variety of issues might be expected to influence plea-bargaining patterns, including

- the defendant's criminal history, especially of violent offenses
- the availability of resources, as measured through employment status or the retention of a private attorney
- the quantity of the drug present at arrest
- the type of drug present at arrest.

In addition, differences in prosecution patterns across counties might be expected because county district attorneys typically have great latitude to determine prosecution policies and procedures.

According to prosecutors, the drug reform sentencing initiatives eliminated the threat of incarceration as a bargaining chip. Thus, analysts foresaw two potential prosecutorial reactions to the initiative (Riley et al., 2000):

- *An increase in possession-for-sale charges.* Under Proposition 36, all cases involving simple possession alone are to draw probation and treatment, but cases involving "possession for sale" are ineligible.[9] Arizona's proposition includes first- and second-time possession, use, or paraphernalia cases and excludes cases of possession for sale, and production, manufacturing, or transportation for sale. Thus, prosecutors may engage in upcharging to possession for sale if they believe that simple possession offenders have criminal histories that do not merit the release to community-based treatment that Proposition 36 provides.
- *An increase in the number of cases with co-occurring charges filed.* In many cases, although it is possible to charge a defendant with a variety of offenses, only the more serious charges or those most likely to "stick" are actually brought. An alternative to upcharging would be increasing efforts to prosecute offenders on all charges filed, even those with less likelihood to result in a conviction at trial.

Research on California's proposition has provided some insight on implementation and impact. For example, a study by Speiglman, Klein, Miller, and Noble (Speiglman et al., 2003) that relied on interviews with key county-based informants from eight counties identified no instances of prosecutorial overcharging in order to make defendants ineligible for treatment. The study did find variation across counties in prosecutors' willingness to negotiate and/or drop charges. With potentially fewer opportunities to bargain, the number of defendants opting for trials did not increase, according to key officials.

In this report, we set out to explore what factors, if any, consistently emerge as predictors of plea-bargaining practices. We would expect that the factors noted above would be significant predictors of plea-bargaining practices.

---

[9] "Possession for sale" is not defined in Proposition 36 and does not exist in the California penal code.

Impact of Proposition 200 in Arizona

In Arizona, the number of prison commitments involving drug related offenses has changed over the past ten years in a way that, on the surface, might be linked to Proposition 200. Figure 1.2 shows that the number of prison commitments involving drug possession increased from 1991 to 1996 (484 to 957) and decreased from 1997 to 2000 (755 to 504). While prison commitments for drug paraphernalia were also increasing from 1991 to 1995 (135 to 322), there was a substantial growth in these cases from 1996 to 1998 (299 to 599). In fact, the increase in paraphernalia cases during the same time that drug possession cases were declining has been viewed as one way to circumvent the mandate of mandatory drug treatment for drug offenders.

Figure 1.2
Total Arizona Prison Commitments of Drug Offenders

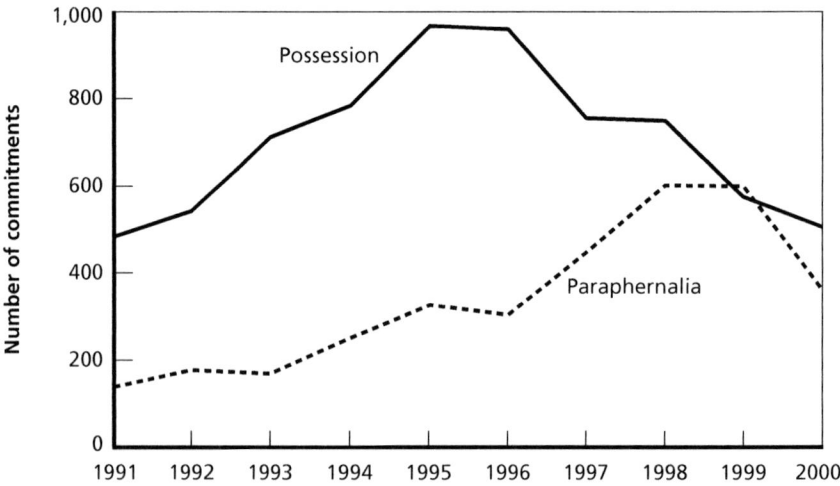

We capitalize on Arizona's longer experience with the effects of the drug proposition to explore the implications of these patterns and, specifically, what kinds of adjustments the criminal justice system makes after implementation of the initiative.

CHAPTER TWO

Study Design and Methodology

This chapter briefly describes California's and Arizona's definitions of low-level drug offender in the context of this study and describes the other methodological elements of the study.

The Definition of Low-Level Drug Offenses

For the California portion of the study, the definition of low-level drug offenses was in part derived from the proposition and in part from California statutes. The proposition specifically included the unlawful possession; use of any controlled substance identified in §11054, §11055, §11056, §11057, or §11058 of the Health and Safety (H&S) Code; or the offense of being under the influence of a controlled substance in violation of §11550 of the H&S Code. For purposes of this study, these conviction offenses are considered low-level charges. We also identified the statutes that appeared to apply to the propositions and separately labeled those offenses to enable comparison to the offenses specifically mentioned in Proposition 36.

Some charges appear to be low level but were not included in the language of the initiative. An example is P4573.8—unauthorized possession of drugs or alcoholic beverages in prison, camp, jail, etc. We count these offenses as low level and track them separately in the event that they have distinguishable analytic outcomes associated with them.

Arizona's Proposition 200 applied to cases involving possession or use of a controlled substance. As previously noted, subsequent case law made paraphernalia cases eligible for mandatory drug treatment. Given this change, low-level drug offenses in Arizona included drug possession, use, and paraphernalia offenses. (See the appendix, Classification of California and Arizona Drug Offenses, for a full listing of offense classifications.)

Identification of Sample

California Population

Study Universe. The *universe* is defined as defendants imprisoned on a low-level drug offense as the most serious charge and tried in one of the nine counties in California with the largest offender population, during 1998 and 1999, the two years preceding Proposition 36. Using records from the California Department of Corrections (CDC), we identified more than 23,000 imprisoned California offenders as having met the specified criteria. Those committed in 1998 and 1999 were chosen in anticipation that both the incarceration and prosecution records would be complete yet current and relatively easily available. We focused on new prison commitments and excluded parole revocations because returns to custody are administrative processes that rarely involve prosecutors. However, we did include probation violators since prosecutors are typically involved in the probation revocation process. We had aimed to gather data from the counties in California with the largest prison population of low-level drug offenders. These included Alameda, Los Angeles, Orange, Riverside, Sacramento, San Bernardino, San Diego, San Francisco, and Santa Clara Counties. San Francisco County declined to participate, citing the low likelihood that the study would produce anything of benefit for drug offenders. Kern County, which is a populous county north of Los Angeles and home to a large population of methamphetamine users, was added after San Francisco's refusal. Ultimately, we were unable to obtain data from Sacramento County (some data that were available electronically could not be aligned with abstracted data from other counties), Orange County (concerns about confidentiality), and San Bernardino County (also concerns about confidentiality).

Sampling Procedures. Our analytical goals included assessing differences by many factors including county, drug type, and race of the offender. The sampling plan, therefore, required balancing the objectives of all the analyses that we planned to consider. For example, in order to distinguish the rates of plea-bargaining across races, the optimal sampling strategy (assuming roughly equal plea-bargaining rates in each group) is to sample equal numbers of offenders in each of the race groups. A sample generated with such a sampling strategy might limit the questions we could answer about differences across counties or across drug types since offenders of a particular race might be underrepresented in some counties or rarely be charged with particular drug offenses.

The aim of our sampling plan was to generate a sample so that we could estimate rates and averages with similar precision for all subpopulations of interest. For the California sample, a *subpopulation* was defined as a collection of offenders having the same race (4 levels), sex (2 levels), county (6 levels), and offense type (5 levels). Some combinations of these four characteristics were more frequent than others. Eighty-five of the 240 ($4 \times 2 \times 6 \times 5$) subpopulations had no subjects in them and many others had only one or two. For example, there were very few offenders in prison on marijuana offenses; Kern, Riverside, and Santa Clara counties had no black marijuana offenders. The sampling plan allocated the greatest sampling effort to those subpopulations with the largest number of offenders. The fundamental strategy was to sample incrementally from the subpopulation for which we had the least amount of precision.

The *effective sample size* (ESS) is the number of observations in a simple random sample that we would need to select from an infinite population to have the same precision as we would have with a sample of n from our sampling plan. The ESS is a convenient measure for the information we can obtain from a subpopulation. We denote the size of the jth subpopulation of the offenders with N_j. From subpopulation j we will randomly selected n_j offenders. The effective sample size for estimating statistics associated with sub-population j is

$$\text{ESS}_j = \frac{n_j(N_j - 1)}{N_j - n_j}.$$

If $n_j = 0$, then $\text{ESS} = 0$, indicating that we have no information on that subpopulation. If we select all of the observations from a sub-population ($n_j = N_j$), then ESS is infinite, indicating that we have perfect information for that subset of offenders.[1] We utilized ESS to flag the subpopulation for which we had the least amount of information. Any additional sampling effort should be allocated to that sub-population. For example, subpopulations with no sampled offenders ($n_j = 0$) have $\text{ESS} = 0$, indicating that these subpopulations are first in line for any additional sampling effort.

The above analysis lays the groundwork for the algorithm we used to generate both the California and Arizona samples. The first step defined the various subpopulations of interest. For California, we defined the subpopulations according to

- race (black, Latino, white, and other)
- offense (depressant, marijuana, narcotic, non-narcotic, and of-fenses for which Proposition 36 might apply in part)
- county (Alameda, Kern, Los Angeles, Orange, Riverside, Sacra-mento, San Bernardino, Santa Clara, and San Diego)[2]
- sex.

Once the subpopulations were defined, we counted the number of offenders in each category to obtain N_j. Second, we set $n_j = 0$ to ini-tialize the process. Third, we computed the ESS for each subpopula-tion. For each subpopulation with the smallest ESS (several may be

---

[1] If $N_j = 0$ or $N_j = n_j = 1$, then ESS is defined to be infinity.

[2] These were the counties originally intended to be part of the study. As discussed above, not all participated.

tied for the smallest) we increased n_j by one. We then recomputed ESS for each subpopulation, again identified those with the smallest ESS, incremented their n_j's by one, and repeated this process until the sum of the n_j's equaled 1,500. This process iteratively allocated our budgeted sampling effort to those subpopulations for which we had the least amount of information. Finally, we drew the actual sample, randomly selecting n_j offenders from subpopulation j, recording their ID numbers, and forwarding the lists to the data collectors.

We would have preferred to stratify by drug type, but California drug codes are generally not drug-specific, except for marijuana. We could not discover the type of drug associated with the offender until we pulled the prosecution records. In hopes of generating a diversity of drug types in the sample, we stratified by offense codes grouped according to the types of drugs that could be associated with the offense codes. One of the categories includes all codes that our legal analysis indicated that Proposition 36 might cover "in part." In the population, 46 percent of the offense codes fell into the narcotic category and 30 percent into the non-narcotic category. Twenty-four percent were covered in part by Prop 36, and a fraction of a percent involved depressant and marijuana cases.

In California, we fell short of our goal of 1,500 subjects. We were unable to acquire data from Sacramento, Orange, and San Bernardino Counties. Our final sample contained 875 offenders. We computed sampling weights so that the weighted sample matched the population from the six counties by race, sex, and primary offense category.

Arizona Population

In Arizona, we sought a sample that encompasses the pre- and post-implementation periods. Given that there were substantial challenges to the Arizona initiative immediately after its passage, we believe that prosecutorial behavior may have changed continuously for many years.[3] Thus, we needed multiple years of Arizona data, rather than a simple before-and-after sample. Given that the implementation of Arizona Proposition 200 took place in Fiscal Year (FY) 1998 (July 1997 to June 1998), we have chosen to use commitments to the Arizona Department of Corrections (AZDOC) from FY 1997 through FY 2000 that involved use, possession, and paraphernalia cases.

To capture the prosecution processes of low-level drug offenses before and after the implementation of Proposition 200, the population of low-level drug offenders committed to the Arizona Department of Corrections from 1996 to 2000 was obtained from the AZDOC. The population of such offenders comprised 4,931 low-level drug commitments. Because Maricopa, Pima, Mohave, and Yuma counties were responsible for 89 percent of all drug commitments to the AZDOC, the sample was drawn from these four counties. We determined that 400 cases per year would yield the ability to detect a 10 percent difference in proportion means with more than 80 percent probability for a factor with four categories (i.e., four counties). A sample size of 1,600 cases produced excellent power for factors (e.g., criminal history, type of drug, race/ethnicity, and gender) with a low number of categories. The sample allocation strategy proceeded in the same fashion as described previously for California. For Arizona, however, we defined the subpopulations by race, offense, county, sex, and year of imprisonment. As with California, we computed sampling weights so that the weighted sample matched the population in terms of county, drug type, race/ethnicity, and gender.

---

[3] This is especially important given that up until a recent Arizona Supreme Court decision (see *State v. Estrada*, No. CR-00-0140-PR and No. CR-00-0306 PR Ariz. Nov. 15, 2001), two state courts of appeals in 1998 and 2000 delivered conflicting decisions on the applicability of mandatory drug treatment in paraphernalia cases (*State v. Holm*, 195 Ariz. 42, 985 P.2d 527, and *State v. Estrada*, 197 Ariz. 383, 4 P.3d 438).

Data Collection Procedures

Instrumentation and Training

Instrument Development. The California and Arizona teams jointly identified a core set of constructs and variables of analytic interest. The constructs served as the basis for development of the data abstraction form. The constructs and variables were organized into fields within the data abstraction form, which included offender demographics, arrest information, prosecution information, disposition information, and criminal history. Project staff from California and Arizona collaborated on the development of the data abstraction form in order to standardize the form where possible. The data abstraction form was pilot-tested within each county to ensure the availability of the variables within the prosecution files. An accompanying data abstraction key and instruction manual were developed that operationalized each field and specified the coding appearing on the form.

Data Abstractor Recruitment and Training. Data abstractors were recruited from a pool of data collectors previously used by RAND researchers and from job postings directed toward local universities with graduate programs in criminal justice or like majors. The California team identified a data abstractor for each county, except that in one instance the same data abstractor was used for two counties. Data abstractors were individually trained by project staff on the use of the data abstraction form and other supplemental documents (e.g., abstraction key and instruction manual). Additionally, each data abstractor was introduced to the various sections within the prosecutor's case file and showed how the information within these sections were linked to the fields within the data abstraction form. The training culminated with the data abstractor completing two to three data abstraction forms in the presence of project staff to gain confidence in completing the form and to provide real-time feedback on abstracting the necessary data. Each data abstractor was introduced to the person to contact within the district attorney's office should any questions arise.

The data collection process proceeded similarly in Arizona. Arizona data collectors were selected from a pool of graduate students and staff with prior experience in collecting court, probation, and booking data. They were trained in the use of the data collection protocol and supervised by the Arizona research team.

California Data

Concurrent with identification of low-level drug prisoners, we attempted to obtain the involvement of the prosecutors responsible for the cases. Shortly after the project received funding, the project staff briefed the California District Attorneys' Association (CDAA) on the effort. CDAA agreed to endorse our requests to have access to the prosecution information from each of the nine counties where we originally anticipated working. The principal investigator wrote a letter to each of the district attorneys (DAs) asking for their participation in the project, and that letter was followed by a letter of endorsement from CDAA.

Although most district attorneys were interested in supporting the project, several problems emerged in the first few months. First, many DAs felt that they did not have the authority to provide access to the files because of state statutes that governed access to confidential information. Ultimately, it was determined that there were research exemptions to these data restrictions. However, since the California Attorney General's (AG's) office was responsible for prosecuting violations of the statutes, some DAs wanted a letter from the AG's office that gave them permission to participate in the study. Since the AG's office had not requested the study, we first had to convince the AG's office that the project represented a legitimate research undertaking. Eventually, these issues were resolved in most of the counties where we wanted to collect data, though at a cost of several months of delay.

In the interim, three counties refused, or ultimately were unable, to participate. San Francisco officials did not believe that the study would provide benefit for their offender population. Orange County declined to participate because of concerns about the state's confidentiality statutes and because it did not have staff to supervise the data collection process. San Bernardino County declined for similar reasons. Among the counties that participated, several required that the data collection staff undergo background investigations before they were permitted to have access to the records.

Among the counties that participated, we did not collect the expected sample size (see Table 2.1). There were a variety of reasons for the shortfall in sample size achievement, including the inability to locate files, the provision of the wrong files, and vital information missing from files.

Once the county participation was secured, we engaged the assistance of another stakeholder, the California Department of Corrections (CDC). The CDC identified the universe of offenders incarcerated on a low-level drug offense at California correctional institutions between January 1, 1998, and December 31, 1999. This pool of offenders constituted the universe of offenders from which we derived our study sample for each of the participating counties.

Table 2.1
Expected and Achieved Sample Sizes in California

County	Expected	Completed	Outstanding
Alameda	119	114	5
Kern	182	153	29
Los Angeles	217	194	23
Riverside	159	125	34
San Diego	198	154	44
Santa Clara	141	138	3

Arizona Data

Various strategies were employed to acquire prosecution data for imprisoned low-level drug offenders. The Arizona Department of Corrections provided electronic data on offenders' demographics (i.e., gender, race/ethnicity), state and federal identification numbers, arrest dates, sentencing states, state admission dates, jurisdiction of case, drug type, and sentence length. To obtain criminal history records, the principal investigators signed a nondisclosure agreement with the Arizona Department of Public Safety and received approval to obtain electronic data on criminal histories for all offenders in the sample. After a review of the data that were provided electronically, a condensed data abstraction form was constructed. This form was utilized to collect data from prosecution case files. Thus, forms were used to collect arrest specific information, probation status, prosecution charging information, and sentencing outcome data.

Data abstraction from case files was started in Maricopa County in November 2002. Staff from the county attorney's office reviewed the low-level drug cases needed for the study and determined that the majority of publicly available prosecution files had been destroyed in accordance with their file destruction schedule and that access to nonpublic files was required. The Maricopa County Attorney's office then facilitated access, through a court order, to review nonpublic case files from the Maricopa County Clerk's office. Data abstraction was coordinated with the clerk's office, and trained researchers began the data collection process in March 2003 and completed it in May 2003. During the data collection process, officials in the county clerk's office informed researchers that the data being collected from court files were routinely submitted to the Arizona Department of Corrections. After consultation and confirmation from the Arizona Department of Corrections that such data were kept in the department's case files, arrangements were made to collect data from state commitment files for cases from the other counties (Pima, Mohave, and Yuma counties). Data collection at AZDOC began on June 15, 2003, and was completed on July 30, 2003.

Measures

California Measures

Offense Severity Index. For every offense code in California criminal law, the California Bureau of Criminal Statistics has assigned a severity score ranging between 1 and 74, with lower numbers representing more severe offenses. Murder, for example, is the most severe offense in California criminal law, with a severity score of 1. Serious offenses against persons (e.g., rape, robbery, kidnapping) are rated 1–7; major property crimes such as burglary or forgery, 8–11; major drug felonies (e.g., possession of narcotics or drug trafficking), 12–16. Misdemeanor drug offenses are assigned severity scores of 34–36. Examples of severity scores for less serious offenses include trespassing (49), possession of burglary tools (61), and driving with a suspended license (74). For each offense in the criminal history of our California sample, including all offenses in the current arrest, we assigned a corresponding severity score.

Using the severity score for past arrests and conviction, we were thus able to determine the most severe prior arrest offense, as well as the most severe conviction offense. Likewise, if there were multiple charges in the most current arrest, we were able to determine the most severe charge for the case as a whole. For analytic purposes, we reversed the scale so that higher severity scores were associated with more severe offenses. To summarize the severity of a group of charges (e.g., criminal history, filed charges) we computed the sum severity score of those charges.

Criminal History. We assessed criminal history by capturing each offender's prior offense arrests and offense convictions covering the seven years preceding the most recent arrest. For analytic purposes, we converted prior arrests and convictions using the same methodology as we used to define the severity index. Additionally, criminal history was reflected as the total number of prior arrests and convictions.

Plea-Bargaining. We expressed plea-bargaining as a measure of distance along the severity index between arrest charges and charges at conviction. Pleading-down was operationalized as having moved down the severity index during the interval between arrest charges and charges at conviction. We computed the severity of arrest, filing, and conviction charges as the sum of the severities of the individual charges. Additionally, we recorded whether there was a plea deal, which was defined as having the original offense(s) dropped or where in the file there was an indication of a plea. In Arizona, plea-bargaining occurred between the arrest and the filing of charges; in

California plea-bargaining occurred after the charges were filed but before sentencing.

Sociodemographic Characteristics. We conceptualized race, age, gender, employment status, and county as background characteristics potentially associated with drug prosecution. "Race" was recorded as white, black, Asian, Latino, Native American, or other, which are based on the categories used by the CDC. "Age" was recorded as the age on the date of arrest. "Gender" was recorded as male or female. "Employment status" was recorded as yes or no based on whether the offender was employed at the time of arrest. Employment data will help provide indication both of socioeconomic status (SES) and the offender's functioning. "County" represents the county in which the offender was arrested, serves as a proxy for prosecutor practices, and controls for potential differences in practices.

Drug Type and Quantity. Drug type was assessed from the arrest information in the prosecution file and was of analytic interest to examine whether offenses for certain types of drugs were differentially prosecuted. We classified the type of drug under possession at the time of arrest using six categories: marijuana, cocaine, heroin, multiple drugs excluding marijuana, multiple drugs including marijuana, and other.

In addition, drug quantity was captured and converted into weight in grams. Some quantities recorded in prosecution records were not in readily convertible terms, such as "PCP cigarette," "syringe of heroin," or "bag of MJ." We developed a drug weight conversion table for these drugs by researching other publicly available drug case files, online drug discussion groups, and official information from the Office of National Drug Control Policy (ONDCP) and the Drug Enforcement Administration (DEA).

Kind of Trial. To control for potential differences between judges and juries in terms of how they view drug offenses, we looked at what kind of trial offenders had. Specifically, we measured whether they had a jury trial or a bench trial.

Arizona Measures

To examine whether imprisoned low-level drug offenders' charges changed before and after Proposition 200, we constructed an implementation period. Identifying a precise implementation period across the state was difficult given that resources and contracts with treatment providers were allocated at different times. According to Arizona's Administrative Office of the Courts, implementation of Proposition 200 began during FY 1998 (July 1, 1997–June 30, 1998). To establish the *implementation period* (pre-implementation = 0; post-implementation = 1), we created various time reference points during the 1998 fiscal year (i.e., July 1997, January 1998, and June 1998) to examine whether time produced any significant differences in plea-bargaining practices pre– and post–Proposition 200. The difference in coefficients and standard errors among models starting at each reference point and continuing through the fiscal year was slight. The June 1998 implementation reference point was selected to ensure that all counties had fully implemented Proposition 200.

To examine the charging and prosecution processes for imprisoned low-level drug offenders, we constructed several measures. First, we created an overall measure of *type of disposition* to capture the extent to which pleading guilty (coded "1") or bench/jury trials (coded "0") took place in low-level drug cases. Second, we utilized an *offense charging* measure to capture whether the number of charges from the arrest (or probation) increased (coded "1"), decreased (coded "2"), or remained the same (coded "3") at the time of prosecution. We also used this measure to identify whether charges changed from prosecution to time of sentencing. Third, we assigned a severity score to all offenders' charges at arrest, prosecution, and sentencing to construct a *sum severity score*.[4] Consistent with the charging measure, the sum severity score from the arrest (or probation) to prosecution and from prosecution to sentencing was assessed to capture whether the score increased (coded "1"), decreased (coded "2"), or remained the same (coded "3") from one stage to the next.

---

[4] As in California, this score was inverted to facilitate interpretation and enable its use as a dependent variable.

Study objectives included exploring how criminal histories, drug type, gender, and race/ethnicity influenced the plea-bargaining processes. Given the important role that prior record plays in the sentencing process, we analyzed several criminal history measures.[5] These measures include the number of *prior arrests* and *prior offenses* in criminal record. We also constructed a *sum severity score of prior offense*. We created a *probation status* (probationers = 1; arrestees = 0) measure to distinguish imprisoned offenders who were arrested for a drug offense(s) from those who were under probation supervision at the time of sentencing. *Drug offense* was measured by using a set of five indicator variables (marijuana, dangerous drug, narcotic drug, vapors, and paraphernalia) and *drug type* by using a set of seven indicator variables (marijuana, cocaine, crack, heroin, methamphetamine, vapors, and paraphernalia). To capture the extent to which incarcerated low-level drug offenders were originally arrested for the sale, distribution, or trafficking of drugs, we created a *drug sale* (yes = 1; no = 0) measure.[6] The possession of a *gun* or *knife* (yes = 1; no = 0) during the commission of the offense was also analyzed. Factors of interest, including offenders' *gender* (male = 1; female = 0), *race/ethnicity* (a set of five indicator variables: white, black, Latino, Native American, race-other), *age* (at sentencing), *employment status* (yes = 1; no = 0), and *county* (a set of four indicator variables: Maricopa, Pima, Mohave, and Yuma counties) were collected and included in the analyses.

---

[5] Several criminal history measures, including arrest, were needed because of doubts about the completeness of the prior-offense data. Criminal history rap sheets provided by the Arizona Department of Public Safety, the state agency responsible for maintaining offenders' criminal histories, included prior arrests and convictions. Officials indicated that, because they maintain only data submitted to their office, these data are by no means a valid measure of offenders' prior criminal activity. For example, although convictions should be submitted to this state agency, not all jurisdictions provide such data. Based on informal discussions with agency officials, they indicated that approximately 70 percent of all arrest data lack a disposition outcome, making convictions in these data an *underestimate* of offenders' true prior convictions.

[6] Although drug quantity was collected from case files, the classification and conversion of these data into one unit (e.g., grams) was made difficult by the numerous descriptions of drug quantities in police arrest reports. As a result, drug sale charges were used to measure the extent to which drug quantity influenced plea-bargaining outcomes.

CHAPTER THREE

Drug Prosecutions Resulting in Imprisonment in the Pre-Proposition Eras

Low-Level Drug Offenders in California

Population Description

Table 3.1 presents a description of the California sample in total ("population" column) and separately by whether the imprisonment resulted from an arrest or probation violation. The California population consisted primarily of male offenders. Nearly three out of four of the offenders were not employed at the time of their arrest. The population was fairly evenly distributed across racial and ethnic groups. Approximately one-third were black, one-third were Latino, and slightly more than one-quarter were white. In addition, almost 30 percent were probation offenders.

Among arrestees (i.e., excluding probationers), nearly 50 percent of the cases involved cocaine, 10 percent involved heroin, and less than 3 percent involved marijuana only. An additional 5 percent of the cases involved multiple drugs including marijuana, and 4 percent involved multiple drugs but no marijuana.

Drug sale, transportation, and importation cases (at arrest) constituted 7 percent of all cases and 25 percent of the conviction cases. Pleading guilty was overwhelmingly used for disposition of cases (98 percent). Probationers and arrestees seldom utilized bench and jury

Table 3.1
**Description of Imprisoned Low-Level Drug Offenders
in California, Pre–Proposition 36**

	Population	Probationers	Arrestees
Number	875	256 (29%)	619 (71%)
Gender, %			
Male	85	80	86
Female	15	20	14
Race/ethnicity, %			
White	28	20	25
Latino	35	38	34
Black	34	40	38
Race-Other	3	2	3
Average age at sentencing in years (SD[a])	35.2 (9.2)	33.1 (9.4)	35.4 (9.0)
Employed, %			
Yes	29	23	32
No	71	77	68
County, %			
Alameda	3	8	2
Kern	8	7	9
Los Angeles	62	72	58
Riverside	8	4	10
San Diego	15	6	18
Santa Clara	4	3	5
On probation %			
Yes	29	—	—
No	71	—	—
Drug type, %			
Cocaine	53	65	48
Heroin	8	3	10
Marijuana only	3	3	2
Multiple, including MJ[b]	5	5	5
Multiple, excluding MJ	4	4	4
Other	27	19	30
Drug sale, %			
Yes	25	22	26
No	75	78	74
Prop 36 applies, %			
Yes	75	78	73
Partially	24	21	25
Arguably no	2	<1	2

Table 3.1—continued

	Population	Probationers	Arrestees
Mode of disposition, %			
Pled guilty	98	99	97
Bench trial	0.3	0.0	0.4
Jury trial	2	0.5	2
	Average (SD)	Average (SD)	Average (SD)
Currency at arrest	$214 ($2,222)	$87 ($270)	$260 ($2,591)
Number of arrest/ probation charges	11.1 (9.1)	7.6 (7.3)	12.5 (9.4)
Number of arrests in prior record	8.7 (6.8)	6.2 (0.7)	9.8 (7.1)
Number of offenses in prior record	3.4 (3.1)	2.0 (0.3)	3.9 (3.2)
Sum severity score of prior offense	167.1 (8.9)	98.8 (115.6)	194.8 (158.9)
Number of charges filed by prosecution	2.9 (0.1)	1.8 (1.1)	3.4 (1.8)
Sum severity score of charges filed by prosecution	128.7 (5.7)	76.1 (46.8)	150.0 (89.2)
Number of charges at sentencing	1.3 (0.7)	1.2 (0.5)	1.3 (0.8)
Sum severity score of offenses at sentencing	62.3 (44.2)	53.0 (26.8)	66.1 (49.1)
Sentence length (in months)	30.8 (15.0)	34.2 (12.1)	29.4 (15.8)

NOTES: These figures were calculated using the sample weighted to match the population. The analogous table describing the Arizona data (Table 3.14) reports some different prior-record statistics than we show here for California. In Arizona, conviction data were unreliable and were not used for assessing criminal history.
[a] SD = standard deviation.
[b] MJ = marijuana.

trials. Table 3.1 also describes the offenders' records in terms of prior arrests, number of arrests and conviction charges past and present, and the average severity of those charges.

Table 3.2 summarizes several measures of criminal history and criminality, including the number of arrest charges, number of prior arrests, and prior conviction history (number and severity score). The California offenders had an average of 9.8 prior arrests and 3.9 prior convictions in their record (with a sum severity score of 195 for prior

Table 3.2
Summary of Arrest, Prosecution, Conviction, and Sentencing History and Severity—California Drug Offenders

	Mean	SE[a]
Number of prior arrests	9.8	0.52
Number of prior convictions	3.9	0.21
Average total severity of prior convictions	194.8	10.56
Average severity score of most severe conviction	55.5	1.49
Average number of arrest charges	1.9	0.09
Average number of charges filed at prosecution	3.4	0.13
Average number of sentencing charges	1.3	0.04
Average prison sentence (months)	29.4	1.43

[a] SE = standard error.

offenses). Low-level drug offenders had an average of 3.4 charges filed by prosecutors. On average, low-level drug offenders in the sample were sentenced to prison for 29.4 months pre–Proposition 36.

In terms of the sample, Proposition 36 appeared to apply to nearly three-quarters (73 percent) of the arrestees in the population. It partially or arguably applied to about 25 percent of the cases. Proposition 36 had no application to about 2 percent of the cases, although these instances were still defined by the study team as low-level offenses.

Prosecution Resulting in Imprisonment for Possession Offenders

Prior Drug and Other Offenses. By offense type, 68 percent of those in prison on a sales charge have a previous drug conviction, and 78 percent of them have a previous conviction of some sort. Among those in prison on charges other than sales offenses, 72 percent have a previous drug charge conviction and 98 percent have a previous criminal conviction of some sort. The fact that non-sales convictions are more likely to be associated with previous drug or other convictions suggests that criminal history plays a role in the prosecution of non-sales offenses.

Pleading from Sales to Non-Sales. Overall, a relatively small percentage of those in prison on possession charges pled down from a sales charge. Of the offenders in prison on something other than a sales charge, 11 percent were originally charged with a drug sale or transport offense (see Table 3.3). Marijuana offenders appear no more or less likely to plead down from a sales to non-sales charge than are offenders involved with other drugs. Thus, with some variation by drug (presented in Table 3.3), about 1 in 10 possession convictions appears to result from plea arrangements that result in dropped sales or transportation charges. The balance originated and ended as non-sales charges.

Table 3.4 shows that for the cases that involved a sales charge at arrest and conviction, an average of 200 grams of drugs was present at arrest. In contrast, for the cases that involved sales at arrest, but possession at conviction, an average of 126 grams of drugs was present. Finally, for cases that began and ended as possession offenses, an average of nearly 74 grams of drugs was present. There seem to be clear quantitative breaks between sales and non-sales cases. Instances

Table 3.3
Percentage of Non-Sales Convictions Originating with Sales or Transport Charges

Drug Type	Originally a Sales or Transport Charge, %	Standard Error
Cocaine	11	3.6
Heroin	1	0.9
Marijuana	13	9.6
Multiple including MJ	22	8.8
Multiple excluding MJ	8	4.4

Table 3.4
Average Quantity of Drugs,
by Sales and Non-Sales Charges and Convictions

Sale Charge?	Sale Conviction?	Average Quantity (gm)	Standard Error
Yes	Yes	200.2	15.4
Yes	No	126.3	19.5
No	No	74.3	6.0

involving large amounts of drugs (200 grams and over) are likely to start out and remain sales cases, whereas instances involving smaller amounts of drugs are less likely to start out as sales cases.

Criminal Histories of Sales and Non-Sales Offenders. On average, those imprisoned on non-sales charges have more severe criminal histories than those imprisoned on sales offenses. As demonstrated in Tables 3.5 and 3.6, this pattern holds up across drug types and, generally, across counties. Specifically, Tables 3.5 and 3.6 show that regardless of the type of drug involved or where an offender is prosecuted, imprisoned non-sales offenders have more severe criminal histories than imprisoned sales offenders.

Table 3.5
Criminal History by Sales, Non-Sales Offense, and Drug Type

Sales Offense?	Total Criminal History Severity	Standard Error	Number of Convictions in Criminal History	Standard Error
Cocaine				
No	202	23.2	4.0	0.44
Yes	159	20.3	3.2	0.43
Heroin				
No	196	26.3	4.2	0.43
Yes	46	31.9	1.0	0.69
Marijuana				
No	211	75.2	4.7	1.54
Yes	117	25.3	1.9	0.41

Table 3.6
Criminal History by Sales, Non-Sales Offense, and County

Sales Offense?	Total Criminal History Severity	Standard Error	Number of Convictions in Criminal History	Standard Error
Alameda				
No	332	124.9	5.8	2.03
Yes	97	20.6	1.7	0.36
Kern				
No	259	35.8	5.4	0.71
Yes	137	41.9	2.8	0.86
Los Angeles				
No	197	20.1	4.1	0.39
Yes	128	19.3	2.4	0.38
Riverside				
No	219	25.9	4.2	0.46
Yes	210	50.1	3.9	0.81
Santa Clara				
No	272	23.1	5.7	0.52
Yes	182	43.5	3.9	0.93
San Diego				
No	238	19.8	4.6	0.38
Yes	159	26.1	3.2	0.56

Summary of Prosecution of Possession Offenders. In California, there seems to be support for the prosecution contention that the people imprisoned on possession charges have more extensive criminal histories or have cases that involve larger amounts of drugs. Imprisoned non-sales offenders are more likely to have a criminal record or a criminal record involving drugs than sales offenders.

There are very few marijuana offenders in prison. Although our sampling plan targeted marijuana offenders, our final sample contained only 18 such offenders, reducing our ability to infer patterns for these subjects. Our sample included ten marijuana arrestees who ended up in prison (not via a trial). Two of them were sales offenses (§11359 and §11351). The remaining eight convicted on possession charges tended to be in possession of large quantities (261 grams, 251, 237, 145, 105, 71, 66, the last was not recorded). Among the three caught with under 100 grams (or an unknown quantity), all had at least two prior convictions. One of these three offenders had three prior convictions including a strike. Another one of them was also caught with $208 in cash. That leaves one marijuana possessor who seems somewhat unusual, a possessor with no other aggravating circumstances in arrest charges or filing charges but with two prior convictions.

From the information that we do have on marijuana cases, we found that marijuana offenders pled down from a sales to non-sales charge at about the same rates as other offenders, with the exception of heroin offenders, who rarely escaped initial sales charges (shown in Table 3.3). This appears to support arguments that prosecutors may be treating marijuana relatively harshly. In Table 3.4, we saw that cases involving large amounts (200 grams and over) of drugs are likely to start out and remain sales cases, while those instances involving smaller amounts of drugs are less likely to start out as sales cases. As described in more detail in the next section, which focuses more closely on marijuana offenders, marijuana offenders are disproportionately likely to be arrested with more than 200 grams of drugs.

Finally, Tables 3.5 and 3.6 suggest that prosecutors treat sales offenses more harshly and that non-sales offenders must have more severe criminal histories to end up in prison on non-sales charges.

Prosecution Resulting in Prison Terms for Marijuana Offenders

In the entire population eligible for entry into our sample (more than 23,000), there were 27 §11357 (marijuana possession) offenders and 10 §11360(A) (marijuana transportation) offenders.

Previous Drug Convictions. Among arrestees, 71 percent of the prisoners have a previous drug conviction and 92 percent have a previous conviction of one type or another (including drugs). By drug type, 60 percent of imprisoned marijuana offenders have a previous drug conviction of one sort or another, and 79 percent have a prior conviction of some kind (see Table 3.7). In contrast, 70 percent of cocaine offenders have prior drug convictions and 97 percent of them have prior convictions of some kind. Heroin offenders have prior drug convictions in 51 percent of the cases, and prior convictions of any sort in 79 percent of the cases.

Table 3.7
Percentage of Imprisoned Low-Level Drug Offenders with a Previous
Drug Conviction, by Drug

Drug	Prior Drug Convictions	Standard Error	Prior Convictions	Standard Error
Cocaine	70	7.5	97	1.2
Heroin	51	15.6	79	10.6
Marijuana	60	17.7	79	13.2
Multiple including MJ	68	9.5	89	7.0
Multiple excluding MJ	74	9.7	85	7.5
None/unknown	68	19.7	85	11.0
Other	79	4.2	93	2.9

Drug Quantities. Across all imprisonment charges, drug quantity on the offender at arrest varies greatly by the drug. Marijuana offenders frequently are caught with large quantities. Seventy-five percent of marijuana offenders had more than 225 grams at arrest, and the median marijuana offender had 246 grams at arrest. In contrast, cocaine offenders were caught with substantially smaller quantities. Seventy-five percent of cocaine offenders had more than 29 grams at arrest, and the median cocaine offender had 46 grams at arrest.

Criminal History. Cocaine offenders generally have a larger number of criminal convictions than marijuana offenders. On average, cocaine offenders have roughly twice as many criminal convictions in their history as marijuana offenders (see Table 3.8).

In addition, as shown in Table 3.9, marijuana offenders on average have a lower criminal history score than cocaine offenders. Note that all of these measures are necessarily correlated. Marijuana offenders also have fewer arrest charges and fewer arrests in their history.

Plea-Bargaining. Marijuana offenders are highly likely to be involved in a plea-bargain (see Table 3.10). In contrast, offenders involved with other drug types are typically not as likely to be involved in a plea-bargain. For example, only 70 percent of heroin offenders and 89 percent of cocaine offenders have plea-bargaining action associated with their cases.

Table 3.8
Marijuana and Cocaine Offenders, by Prior Drug Conviction Status

Marijuana Offenders				
Prior Drug Convictions?	Total	Standard Error	Number of Criminal Convictions	Standard Error
No	102	63.1	1.7	1.02
Yes	131	4.9	2.1	0.09
Cocaine Offenders				
No	170	27.8	3.1	0.52
Yes	201	23.6	4.1	0.46

Table 3.9
Conviction and Arrest History, by Drug

Drug	Criminal History Score	SE	Number of Prior Convictions in History	SE	Number of Prior Arrest Charges	SE	Number of Prior Arrests	SE
Cocaine	190	17.5	4	0.3	12	1.1	11	0.9
Heroin	154	23.0	3	0.5	10	1.9	8	1.8
Marijuana	119	24.1	2	0.4	7	1.4	5	0.9
Multiple (with MJ)	189	22.2	4	0.5	13	1.6	8	1.0
Multiple (no MJ)	245	61.7	5	1.4	15	3.3	11	2.0
None/ Unknown	290	70.6	6	1.2	20	3.1	14	2.8
Other	215	15.7	4	0.3	14	0.9	10	0.6

Prosecution of Marijuana Offenders. Overall, there is mixed evidence about whether marijuana offenders are treated more harshly than other drug offenders. On the one hand, marijuana offenders typically have a lower criminal history score, fewer arrest charges, and fewer arrests in their history than cocaine offenders. This is counter to the prosecution hypothesis that an arrestee has to be "bad" (i.e., have a severe criminal history) to be prosecuted on a marijuana offense. On the other hand, severity scores of marijuana offenders tend to

Table 3.10
Percentage of Offenders with Plea Bargains,
by Drug—Arrestees Only

Drug	Plea Bargain	SE
Cocaine	89	3.2
Heroin	70	17.3
Marijuana	99	0.7
Multiple including MJ	85	5.9
Multiple excluding MJ	93	4.3
None/unknown	30	19.3
Other	79	3.7

drop more between arrest and prosecution than those of other drug offenders.

Among those convicted on a non-sales offense, marijuana offenders have a higher criminal history score (211) than cocaine offenders (202) (see Table 3.5). The direction of this finding seems to support the prosecution argument that marijuana offenders have more severe criminal histories, although the difference between marijuana and cocaine offenders represents about one-fifth of a serious felony. In other words, it is hard to make the claim from these data that marijuana offenders are substantially more hardened in terms of criminal history than cocaine offenders.

These results may be driven by a domination of sales offenses among marijuana arrestees but a mix of offenses among arrestees for other drugs. If that is the case, then the drug quantity issue discussed above may be trumping the kind of drug itself. These issues will be further addressed in the multivariate modeling sections below.

The Role of Race

Table 3.11 assesses the relationship between offense and race/ethnicity and drug type. Although there is a sizable proportion of cases with charge reductions, race does not seem to influence charge reductions (p = 0.63). Drug type does seem to influence charge

Table 3.11
Percentage of Cases with Charge Reduction, by Race and Drug—Arrestees Only

Race	Cocaine	Heroin	MJ	Multiple Drugs Includ. MJ	Multiple Drugs, Exclud. MJ	None or Not Known	Other	All
Black	94	—	—	—	—	—	58	87
Latino	82	87	—	66	—	—	74	81
White	65	67	—	99	—	—	83	81
Other	—	—	—	79	—	—	92	90
All	88	67	99	84	93	—	79	83

NOTE: Cells with no entries had an insufficient number of observations to estimate the rate of charge reductions.

reductions (p < 0.001), with marijuana offenses most frequently resulting in dropped charges (logistic model not shown).

Probationers

Probationers entered our sample if the sentencing charge that caused the revocation of their probation was a low-level drug offense. As shown in Table 3.1, approximately 30 percent of the low-level drug offenders in California were under court supervision (i.e., probation) at the time they were prosecuted for their offense(s). Because these offenders are already under the supervision of the criminal justice system, they may be treated differently for the same offense than other nonprobationers. Thus, we examine the bivariate relationship between criminal history and plea-bargaining for probationers.

Indeed, in 64 percent of the cases, the charges increased from probation revocation to prosecution; they remained unchanged in 36 percent of the cases (see Table 3.12). In contrast, in the overwhelming majority of cases the severity score did not change between prosecution and sentencing.

Since most plea-bargaining activity took place from the time of the probation revocation to prosecution, the analyses in Table 3.13 present the relationship between the three criminal history measures

Table 3.12
Change in Percentage of Offense Charges,
Pre–Proposition 36—Probationers Only

	% Change	SE
Charges from probation to prosecution		
Increased	64	7.0
No change	36	7.0
Decreased	0	NA
Charges from prosecution to sentencing		
Increased	0	NA
No change	96	1.0
Decreased	4	1.0

NOTE: Analysis includes cases where the defendant pled guilty. NA=not applicable.

Table 3.13
Relationship Between Criminal History Record and Sum
Severity Score, Pre–Proposition 36—Probationers Only

	Average	SE
Probation to prosecution: severity score increased		
Number of prior arrests	6.0	0.8
Number of prior offenses	2.0	0.3
Severity score for prior offenses	102.0	17.0
Probation to prosecution: no change		
Number of prior arrests	6.4	1.3
Number of prior offenses	1.9	0.5
Severity score for prior offenses	92.7	25.2
Probation to prosecution: severity score decreased	0	NA

and plea-bargaining outcomes from probation to prosecution. In California, those whose severity score increased between probation revocation and prosecution were broadly comparable to those whose severity score did not change across all three dimensions (mean number of prior arrests, mean number of prior offenses, and mean severity score for prior offenses) shown in Table 3.13.

Low-Level Drug Offenders in Arizona

Population Description

Table 3.14 presents a description of imprisoned low-level drug offenders in Arizona before and after Proposition 200. The discussion in this section focuses on pre–Proposition 200 cases, but we include post–Proposition 200 statistics for comparison. A complete discussion of post–Proposition 200 cases follows in the next section. Findings are presented for the overall population and subgroups of the population (i.e., probationers and arrestees).

Males made up over three-fourths (81 percent) of the population of low-level drug offenders. The majority of low-level drug offenders were white, followed by Latinos and blacks. The mean age of offenders in the population was approximately 34. The majority of low-level drug offenders (70 percent) were unemployed before Proposition 200. Not surprisingly, Maricopa County, the largest county in the state, prosecuted most of the drug offenders.

Approximately 57 percent of prisoners were on probation (for a low-level drug offense) prior to their imprisonment. Thus, offenders were either incarcerated for committing a technical violation or had committed a new offense while on probation.[1] Before Proposition 200, marijuana cases constituted only 12.7 percent of all imprisoned low-level drug cases; dangerous drug (25 percent), narcotic drug (34 percent), and paraphernalia cases (26 percent) made up the majority of cases. Interestingly, the imprisonment of marijuana and paraphernalia arrestees seems to be more a product of probation viola-

---

[1] In some instances (27 cases pre- and 34 cases post-proposition), probationers were arrested during their term of probation (as evidenced by the arrest record found in the file). Given the unique status of these low-level drug offenders, their cases have been excluded from the analyses.

Table 3.14
Description of Low-Level Drug Offenders in Arizona, Pre– and
Post–Proposition 200

	Population		Probationers		Arrestees	
	Pre-200	Post-200	Pre-200	Post-200	Pre-200	Post-200
Number	949	649	553	390	384	246
Gender, %						
Male	81	80.5	75.6	77.6	87.7	84.5
Female	19	19.5	24.4	22.4	12.3	14.6
Race/ethnicity, %						
White	47.8	50.0	52.0	54.4	42.5	43.2
Latino	31	27.3	27.2	26.2	35.9	29.7
Black	17	18.4	15.9	15.5	18.4	22.1
Native American	3.2	3.2	3.9	3.1	2.2	3.5
Other	1	1.1	1	0.8	1.1	1.6
Average age at sentencing in years (SD)	33.4 (8.32)	33.8 (8.42)	32.0 (7.73)	33.3 (8.37)	35.3 (8.65)	34.2 (8.44)
Employed, %						
Yes	29.9	31.1	32.6	31.8	26.0	29.5
No	70.1	68.9	67.4	68.2	74.0	70.5
County, %						
Maricopa	68.7	66.2	73.3	67.4	64	64.6
Pima	18	22.5	13.5	23.8	23.2	21.2
Yuma	6.3	4.6	6.9	3.9	5.7	5.6
Mohave	7	6.7	6.3	5.0	7.1	8.7
On probation, %						
Yes	56.6	59.7	100	100	—	—
No	43.4	40.3	0	0	—	—
Drug offense, %						
Marijuana	12.7	10.4	14.5	12.1	10.5	8.0
Dangerous drug	24.9	17.2	25.4	16.5	24.2	17.4
Narcotic drug	34	32.8	28.7	25.8	40.7	43.5
Paraphernalia	26.3	38.2	29.3	44.8	22.8	29.3
Vapor	2	1.4	2.1	1	1.9	1.8
Drug sale,[a] %						
Yes	7.4	7.1	—	—	16.7	16.9
No	92.6	92.9	—	—	83.3	83.1
Mode of disposition, %						
Pled guilty	95.7	96.7	99.6	99.5	90.4	92.6
Bench trial	0.9	0.7	0.1	0.1	2.1	1.7
Jury trial	3.4	2.6	0.3	0.5	7.5	5.7

Table 3.14—continued

	Population		Probationers		Arrestees	
	Pre-200	Post-200	Pre-200	Post-200	Pre-200	Post-200
			Average (SD)			
Currency at arrest	—	—	—	—	Median = $138	Median = $20
Term of probation (in months)	—	—	37.7 (6.6)	—	—	—
Number of arrest/ probation charges	2.1 (1.2)	2.1 (1.0)	1.10 (0.3)	1.3 (0.5)	2.09 (1.2)	2.1 (1.0)
Number of arrests in prior record	8.3 (6.9)	10.7 (9.5)	7.52 (6.0)	9.6 (8.2)	9.37 (7.8)	12.4 (11.1)
Number of offenses in prior record	17.1 (13.4)	21.9 (17.7)	14.69 (11.1)	19.8 (16.0)	20.14 (15.4)	25.1 (19.4)
Sum severity score of prior offenses	671.5 (532.7)	840.4 (707.0)	570.12 (443.7)	715.8 (584.9)	804.62 (607.0)	1022.4 (818.0)
Number of charges filed by prosecution	1.5 (0.9)	1.5 (0.7)	1.26 (0.7)	1.3 (0.6)	1.89 (1.1)	1.7 (0.9)
Sum severity score of charges filed by prosecution	65.8 (48.0)	61.8 (34.0)	51.96 (30.7)	54.0 (26.4)	83.52 (58.8)	73.7 (42.1)
Number of charges at sentencing	1.6 (1.0)	1.5 (0.8)	1.26 (0.7)	1.3 (0.6)	1.92 (1.2)	1.8 (1.0)
Sum severity score of offenses at sentencing	65.4 (50.0)	62.6 (36.4)	51.6 (32.1)	53.8 (25.3)	83.1 (61.7)	75.3 (46.1)
Sentence length (in years)	1.9 (1.4)	1.6 (1.0)	1.7 (0.9)	1.4 (0.7)	2.2 (1.8)	1.9 (1.3)

[a] In six cases, drug quantity data were missing and therefore excluded from the analyses.

NOTES: The figures in this table were calculated using the sample weighted to match the population. The analogous table describing the California data (Table 3.1) also reports information on convictions in the offenders' criminal history, which was unreliable in Arizona.

tions rather than new arrests. Drug sale, transportation, and importation cases (at arrest) constituted 7 percent of all cases and 17 percent of the arrest cases. Pleading guilty was overwhelming used for disposition (96 percent). Probationers nearly always pled guilty, whereas arrestees utilized bench and jury trials in 9.6 percent of cases.

To examine criminal record in the most comprehensive manner possible, we utilized several measures of this variable in the analyses. Before Proposition 200, offenders had an average of 8.32 prior arrests and 17.1 prior offenses (with a sum severity score of 671.5 for prior offenses) in their record.[2] Low-level drug offenders had an average of 1.5 charges filed by prosecutors. The number of charges filed by prosecutors and the corresponding sum severity score of those charges changed minimally at disposition. This indicates that case adjustments take place between arrest and prosecution and not after prosecutors file charges. On average, low-level drug offenders in the weighted sample were sentenced to prison for 1.9 years pre–Proposition 200.

Prosecution Resulting in Prison Sentences for Possession Offenders

The classification and analysis of low-level drug offenders in Arizona were exclusive to offenders who were incarcerated for possession or use of drugs and paraphernalia cases. However, some low-level offenders were arrested for more serious drug offenses. Among the Arizona arrestees, 216 offenders (17 percent) were arrested for the sale, transportation, or importation of drugs pre–Proposition 200. Of these, 190 pled guilty to a lesser included offense.[3] Dangerous drug and narcotic drug cases made up more than three-fourths of these drug cases (see Table 3.15). The overwhelming majority of sale, transportation, and importation offenses involved large drug quantities. Narratives from police arrest records presented below reveal quantities such as the following:[4]

---

[2] A single arrest can include multiple offenses.

[3] Lesser included offenses included drug possession and the inclusion of a preparatory offense (e.g., attempt and facilitation). Most prevalent in the sale, transportation, and importation cases was the preparatory offense, facilitation, which made the most serious drug cases (class 2 or 3 felonies) (i.e., those that exceeded threshold amounts) into class 5 and 6 felonies.

[4] In Arizona, unlike in California, the quantities of the drug are not recorded in standard measures. As previously described, empirical analyses involving drug quantities were not possible with the Arizona data.

Table 3.15
Drug Sale Arrests by Drug Type,
Pre–Proposition 200

Drug Type	Drug Sale Arrests (%)
Marijuana	11.6
Dangerous drug	36.8
Narcotic drug	43.2
Paraphernalia	8.4

NOTE: Analysis includes cases where the defendant pled guilty.

- 166 pounds of marijuana and 1/4 kilo of cocaine
- 21 pounds of marijuana and 218.6 grams of meth
- 295 pounds of marijuana, scales, burlap bags, and plastic trash bags
- 1 pound of methamphetamine (meth)
- 173 pounds of marijuana
- 37.99 grams of meth, glass pipe, scale
- sold one pound of meth for $9500 to undercover officer
- 2 pounds of cocaine.

Prisoners appeared to be in possession not only of large drug quantities but also of various drugs. For example, according to police records, offenders were arrested with the following drug quantities:

- 115 grams of meth, 172 grams of marijuana, plus multiple baggies of methamphetamine and marijuana, scales
- 3.85 grams,12.26 grams of cocaine, 50 pounds of marijuana,100 pounds of marijuana, scale, bags, 70 pounds of marijuana
- 27.6 grams of meth, 413.39 grams of marijuana, and unspecified amounts of paraphernalia
- 220 dosages of percodan and 900 dosages of valium.

Only in a few cases were the drug quantities small. Examples include:

- three rolled cigarettes of marijuana, plastic baggie containing marijuana residue
- one ounce of meth, sold to informant on various occasions
- small amount of marijuana, meth, scale
- $20.00 worth of crack
- 1 rock of crack
- several rocks of crack
- 3.14 grams (10 rocks) of crack, a crack pipe, and baking soda.

To assess plea-bargaining activity among low-level drug offenders, we examine cases adjustments at various stages. Given the possible varying plea-bargaining processes that may be unique to probationers or arrestees, we restrict these analyses to arrestees. Findings indicate that most plea-bargaining activity occurred between arrest and prosecution and not after prosecution (see Table 3.16). The number of charges were reduced from arrest to prosecution in 26 percent of cases; the number of charges increased from arrest to prosecution in 11.5 percent. The increases included filing of additional counts (e.g., one count of possession became two counts of possession), the addition of a paraphernalia charge to a possession case, or the addition of a possession charge to a paraphernalia case. In approximately 55 percent of the cases, the sum severity of charges remained the same from arrest to prosecution. The sum severity score decreased from arrest to prosecution in 32 percent of cases and increased from arrest to prosecution in 13 percent. Consistent with findings of offense charging, the sum severity score did not change post-prosecution in the majority of cases.

Given that most case adjustments take place from the time of arrest to prosecution, we examine the relationship between plea-bargaining and prior record during this stage (see Table 3.17). Findings indicate that offenders with the more extensive and serious prior record were more likely to have their charges reduced. Conversely, the less extensive the prior record, the more likely offenders were to have charges added from the time of arrest to prosecution.

Table 3.16
Change in Offense Charges, Pre–Proposition 200—Arrestees Only

	% Change
Charges from arrest to prosecution	
Increased	11.5
No change	62.5
Decreased	26.0
Charges from prosecution to sentencing	
Increased	3.4
No change	95.2
Decreased	1.4
Sum severity score from arrest to prosecution	
Increased	13.1
No change	54.9
Decreased	32.0
Sum severity score from prosecution to sentencing	
Increased	5.4
No change	82.0
Decreased	12.6

NOTE: Analysis includes cases where the defendant pled guilty.

Table 3.17
Relationship Between Criminal History Record and Sum Severity Score, Pre–Proposition 200—Arrestees Only

	Average
Arrest to prosecution: severity score increased	
Number of prior arrests	6.8
Number of prior offenses	18.3
Severity score—prior offenses	694.7
Arrest to prosecution: no change in severity score	
Number of prior arrests	9.7
Number of prior offenses	19.6
Severity score—prior offenses	787.1
Arrest to prosecution: severity score decreased	
Number of prior arrests	10.2
Number of prior offenses	21.6
Severity score—prior offenses	862.7

NOTES: Analysis includes cases where the defendant pled guilty. Average number of prior arrests and average severity scores are significant across charge outcomes ($p < 0.05$).

Prosecution Resulting in Prison Sentences for Marijuana Offenders

As with all arrestees in Arizona, the majority of plea-bargaining activity in marijuana cases occurred between arrest and prosecution (see Table 3.18). Marijuana cases were less likely to have a change in charges or in sum severity score than other drug cases. When case adjustments were made, marijuana offenders had the number of charges and/or severity score drop from arrest to prosecution. Relatively, few marijuana cases (n = 9) were treated more severely during case processing. To examine whether the low percentage of plea-bargaining activity in marijuana cases was attributable to offenders' criminal history records, we present marijuana offenders' criminal histories by plea outcomes in Table 3.19. Findings show the chronic and severe nature of marijuana offenders' prior records. Offenders who did not have charges change from arrest to prosecution had more extensive prior records than offenders with an increase or decrease in

Table 3.18
Plea-Bargaining, Pre–Proposition 200—Marijuana
Arrestees Only

	% Change
Charges from arrest to prosecution	
Increased	6.8
No change	70.5
Decreased	22.7
Charges from prosecution to sentencing	
Increased	0
No change	100
Decreased	0
Sum severity score from arrest to prosecution	
Increased	6.9
No change	69.5
Decreased	23.7
Sum severity score from prosecution to sentencing	
Increased	2.2
No change	97.1
Decreased	0.7

NOTE: Analysis includes cases where the defendant pled guilty.

Table 3.19
Relationship Between Charging and Criminal History
Record, Pre–Proposition 200—Marijuana Arrestees Only

	Average
Arrest to prosecution: charges increased	
Mean number of prior arrests	8.5
Mean number of prior offenses	16.2
Mean sum severity score of prior offenses	716.0
Arrest to prosecution: no change	
Mean number of prior arrests	10.4
Mean number of prior offenses	20.3
Mean sum severity score of prior offenses	742.2
Arrest to prosecution: charges decreased	
Mean number of prior arrests	10.1
Mean number of prior offenses	17.0
Mean sum severity score of prior offenses	692.1

NOTES: Analysis includes cases where the defendant pled
guilty. There were no statistically significant differences in
criminal history measures across charge outcomes.

charges. Although this relationship was not statistically significant (to
some extent it may be attributed to the small numbers), the effect is
in the expected direction.[5]

A review of the most serious marijuana cases (i.e., sale, transportation, and importation cases) shows that drug quantities in these
cases were extensive. A few narratives from police arrest records reveal
the quantities such as the following:

- 223 lbs of marijuana, 59 lbs of marijuana, 30 lbs of marijuana
- 45.9 pounds of MJ
- Ammunition, 492 grams (brick of marijuana), 21 grams of bud
  [marijuana].

_____

[5] It should be noted that marijuana offenders had more extensive criminal history records
than dangerous drug offenders, vapor-related offenders, and paraphernalia offenders. Only
narcotic drug offenders had more extensive prior records than marijuana offenders. We restrict our current presentation to marijuana offenders to highlight their case processing because they are often perceived as less serious drug offenders. Although we could have placed
some analytical focus on paraphernalia cases, given their less severe nature, we made every
attempt to keep the Arizona analyses as consistent as possible with those of California.

The Role of Race

Offense and race/ethnicity-specific analyses were conducted to assess their relationship in plea-bargaining (see Table 3.20). The number of charges from arrest to prosecution decreased in a larger percentage of cases for Latinos convicted of marijuana and dangerous drug offenses than for whites and blacks. Blacks convicted of narcotic drugs had the lowest percentage of cases with a reduction in charges; white offenders experienced the most case adjustments. For example, although there was an increase in charges in a larger proportion of cases for whites convicted of marijuana, dangerous drug, and paraphernalia, charges were dropped for 47 percent of white paraphernalia offenders from arrest to prosecution.

Probationers

As previously noted, the majority of imprisoned low-level drug offenders in Arizona were under court supervision (i.e., probation) at

Table 3.20
Drug Offenses, Race/Ethnicity, and Offense Charging,
Pre–Proposition 200—Arrestees Only

	MJ, (%)	Dangerous Drugs, (%)	Narcotic Drugs, (%)	Paraphernalia, (%)
Whites				
Charges increased	11.8	28.4	9.2	14.8
No change	68.6	46.7	59.8	38.3
Charges decreased	19.6	24.9	31.0	47.0
Blacks				
Charges increased	11.1		12.3	
No change	72.2	100	71.9	77.4
Charges decreased	16.7		15.8	22.6
Latinos				
Charges increased	3.3	11.3	0.5	13.2
No change	68.3	60.6	78.2	73.5
Charges decreased	28.3	28.2	21.3	13.9

NOTES: Analysis includes change in charges from arrest to prosecution and cases where the defendant pled guilty. Vapor-related offenses and cases involving Native Americans and other racial/ethnic groups are not presented here because of their small representation in the overall population of cases.

the time they were prosecuted for their offense(s). Given the various organizational factors that may influence the revocation of probation, we restrict our current analyses of probationers to bivariate analysis of criminal history and plea-bargaining measures. Our findings indicate that in a majority of probation cases (85 percent) the number of charges did not change from probation to prosecution (see Table 3.21). The number of charges increased from probation to prosecution for 13 percent of probationers and decreased at prosecution for only 3 percent of cases.

In addition, the number of probationers' charges from prosecution to sentencing changed minimally. As noted in footnote 1, only 27 probation cases had police arrest records pertaining to an offense committed during the probation term. However, the fact that the number of charges increased from probation to prosecution for 13

Table 3.21
Change in Offense Charges, Pre–Proposition 200—
Probationers Only

	% Change
Charges from probation to prosecution	
Increased	12.6
No change	84.7
Decreased	2.7
Charges from prosecution to sentencing	
Increased	0
No change	99.9
Decreased	0.1
Sum severity score from probation to prosecution	
Increased	17.6
No change	77.4
Decreased	5.0
Sum severity score from prosecution to sentencing	
Increased	1.4
No change	93.4
Decreased	5.1

NOTE: Analysis includes cases where the defendant pled guilty.

percent of probationers indicates that new offenses were committed and that the number of offenders who were on probation and arrested for a new offense was underestimated. A review of probationers' technical violations showed that, although probationers had been arrested during probation, the corresponding official police records were not in offenders' files. Thus, probationers may have been arrested (as noted in the technical violation reasons) and either had additional charges filed by the prosecutors or had their probation revoked for a violation that may have been based on the commission of a new offense. A review of sum severity score reveals similar findings. The majority of cases (77 percent) experienced no change in sum severity score from probation to prosecution. Probationers were more likely to see an increase (18 percent) rather than a decrease (5 percent) in sum severity score of charges.

Since most plea-bargaining activity took place from the time of the probation revocation to prosecution, the analyses in Table 3.22

Table 3.22
Relationship Between Criminal History Record and Sum Severity Score, Pre–Proposition 200—Probationers Only

	Average
Probation to prosecution: severity score increased	
Mean number of prior arrests	9.4
Mean number of prior offenses	19.4
Mean sum severity score of prior offenses	737.4
Probation to prosecution: no change	
Mean number of prior arrests	7.3
Mean number of prior offenses	14.4
Mean sum severity score of prior offenses	555.8
Probation to prosecution: severity score decreased	
Mean Number of prior arrests	5.0
Mean number of prior offenses	8.2
Mean sum severity score of prior offenses	298.4

NOTE: All three criminal history measures are statistically significant across charge outcomes ($p < 0.001$).

present the relationship between the three criminal history measures and plea-bargaining outcomes from probation to prosecution. Findings show that probationers with the fewest and least severe criminal records were more likely to have charges reduced. Conversely, probationers with the more extensive and severe criminal records were more likely to have charges increase. Although not presented here, 55 percent of probationers had their probation reinstated at least once prior to their imprisonment. This indicates the majority of probationers were given the opportunity to remain on probation rather than be imprisoned as a result of noncompliance. Not surprisingly, with the exception of 24 cases pre–Proposition 200, all probation cases involved revocations of probation.

Factors Influencing Plea-Bargaining

Although the descriptive and bivariate analyses provide useful information on the relationship between low-level drug offenders and plea-bargaining, we now turn to multinomial regression analyses of this relationship. In Arizona and California, plea-bargaining occurs at different stages in the prosecution process. In Arizona, plea-bargaining occurs between the arrest and the filing of charges. In California, on the other hand, prosecutors first file the arrest charges and also may file additional charges and enhancements before plea-bargaining begins. As a result, in California negotiated reductions in charges occur between the filing of charges and sentencing. In this section, we restrict our presentation to arrestees and study the change in sum severity score of cases from prosecution to sentencing for California, and from arrest to prosecution for Arizona.

Plea-Bargaining in California

We used logistic regression to study the factors that are associated with decreases in the sum severity score between prosecution and sentencing. Charges never increased during this stage of the prosecution process. We found that age, drug type, county, and the number of charges filed were significantly associated with charge reduction patterns (see Table 3.23). Specifically, older offenders and offenders charged in Santa Clara compared to Alameda County were less likely to experience a charge reduction between prosecution and sentencing. Conversely, marijuana offenders and offenders from Kern, Los Angeles, Riverside, and San Diego Counties were significantly more likely

Table 3.23
Coefficients from a Logistic Regression Model Estimating the Likelihood of a Decrease in Sum Severity Score, Pre–Proposition 36

	Decrease in Severity	
	β	SE
Intercept[a]	−6.718	2.168
Male	−0.270	0.566
Race (reference: Other)		
Latino	−0.008	0.888
Black	1.560	1.008
White	0.671	0.874
Age at sentencing	−0.055*	0.027
Employed	0.473	0.509
Drug Type (reference: Other)		
Cocaine	−0.934	0.572
Heroin	−0.061	0.613
Marijuana	3.004**	1.072
Multiple drugs, including MJ	0.035	1.035
Multiple drugs, excluding MJ	−0.724	1.294
Drug sale charge	0.410	0.623
County (reference: Alameda)		
Kern	2.863*	1.215
Los Angeles	3.738***	1.127
Riverside	3.817**	1.385
Santa Clara	−3.436**	1.228
San Diego	2.704*	1.356
Number of charges filed	2.917***	0.505
Number of prior convictions	0.048	0.052

NOTE: Analysis includes only arrestees.

[a] Reference category includes No change in sum severity score, Women, Other Race, Unemployed, Other drug, No sales charge, and Alameda County.

* $p < 0.05$; ** $p < 0.01$; *** $p < 0.001$.

to experience charge reductions between prosecution and sentencing. In addition, the likelihood of charge reductions increased as the number of charges filed at prosecution increased. Surprisingly, the number of prior convictions was not a significant factor in the likelihood of experiencing charge reductions.

Plea-Bargaining in Arizona

In Arizona, plea-bargaining takes place between the initial arrest and the prosecution filing of charges. Sometimes the number and severity of charges increased during this phase. We used a multinomial logistic regression model to study the factors that influence the likelihood of the severity of charges decreasing, not changing, or increasing (see Table 3.24).

Findings show that males were more likely than females to have a decrease in severity score. Employed offenders were more likely to have charges decrease than unemployed offenders. Dangerous drug and paraphernalia cases were more likely than marijuana cases to have severity score increase and decrease than not change, indicating higher rates of plea-bargaining or case adjustments in those cases. Cases with a drug sale charge at arrest were more likely to have severity score decrease. As the number of counts increased, severity scores were more likely to decrease and less likely to increase. Offenders with more extensive prior records were more likely to have their severity scores decrease than not change. Offenders convicted in Pima County were less likely than offenders in Maricopa County to have severity score decrease, while offenders convicted in Yuma and Mohave Counties were more likely to have a severity score increase than offenders in Maricopa County.[6]

---

[6] Because the Arizona data did not specifically differentiate the type of drug involved, we are unable to determine the relationship between drug type and plea-bargaining in Arizona. It is also important to note that interactive effects were not explored with the Arizona data.

Table 3.24
Multinomial Estimates of Charge(s), Sum Severity Score—Pre–Proposition 200

	Increase in Severity		Decrease in Severity	
	ß (SE)	Exp (ß)	ß (SE)	Exp (ß)
Intercept[a]	5.016 (1.263)		−2.445 (1.028)	
Male	0.499 (0.349)	1.647	0.663* (0.281)	1.941
Latino	−0.507 (0.270)	0.602	−0.387 (0.213)	0.679
Black	−0.650 (0.381)	0.522	−0.102 (0.276)	0.903
Age at sentencing	−0.017 (0.014)	0.983	−0.001 (0.011)	0.999
Employment	−0.109 0.279)	0.897	0.642*** (0.199)	1.900
Dangerous drugs	2.054*** (0.409)	7.799	0.668* (0.315)	1.950
Narcotic drugs	0.288 (0.456)	1.333	0.162 (0.295)	1.176
Drug para-phernalia	1.636*** (0.420)	5.134	0.940** (0.203)	2.560
Drug sale charge	−0.119 (0.383)	1.126	1.811*** (0.271)	6.117
Counts at arrest	−0.727*** (0.175)	0.483	1.119*** (0.108)	3.062
Prior offenses in record	0.013 (0.007)	1.013	0.021** (0.006)	1.021
Pima	0.807 (0.302)	2.241	−1.219** (0.299)	0.295
Yuma	1.283** (0.361)	3.607	−0.269 (0.356)	0.764
Mohave	1.495*** (0.365)	4.459	−0.899 (0.486)	0.407

−2 Log Likelihood = 1385.76

Chi-Square = 505.17; df = 28

NOTE: Analysis includes only arrestees.

[a] Reference category includes no change in sum severity score, Whites, marijuana cases, and Maricopa County.

* $p < 0.05$; ** $p < 0.01$; *** $p < 0.001$; df = degrees of freedom.

Summary and Policy Implications

In the period before the implementation of Proposition 36 in California and Proposition 200 in Arizona, there is evidence to support the hypotheses of prosecutors. Specifically, when drug sales offenders are compared to non-sales offenders, we see that those imprisoned on non-sales charges (primarily possession) in California have more severe criminal histories than those imprisoned on sales charges. This suggests that criminal history is an aggravating factor that helps equalize the severity of sales and non-sales offenses in the eyes of the law.

In contrast, the story on marijuana is more muddied. In California, we found that the small number of marijuana offenders generally had less severe criminal histories (as measured by the number of arrests and convictions and the severity score of arrest charges and convictions). Analysis of drug quantity data in California show that the average marijuana offense involved substantially greater quantities of drugs than did cocaine or heroin offenses. Indeed, the quantities of marijuana were such that there were very few cases of offenders being imprisoned for simple marijuana possession. Thus, quantity may be playing a role in increasing the severity with which marijuana offenders are being treated.

All of these findings are drawn from descriptive and bivariate analyses. Multivariate analysis clarified the picture somewhat. In California we found that older offenders and offenders charged in Santa Clara County were less likely to benefit from charge reductions, while offenders from other counties (Kern, Los Angeles, Riverside, and San Diego) and marijuana offenders were significantly more likely to experience charge reductions. In addition, the greater the number of charges filed at prosecution, the more likely the chance of a charge reduction. Surprisingly, the number of prior convictions was not a significant factor in the likelihood of charges being reduced.

Pre–Proposition 200, nearly 59 percent of Arizona's incarcerated low-level drug offenders were convicted of a dangerous or narcotic drug offense while 26 percent of the state's low-level drug offenders were paraphernalia offenders. With the exclusion of vapor-related cases, marijuana cases represent the smallest proportion of low-level drug cases in Arizona's prisons (12.7 percent pre-proposition and 10.4 percent post-proposition). A qualitative review of drug quantities shows a substantial percentage (about 17 percent) of Arizona's low-level drug offenders were originally arrested for offenses that included sales, transportation, and importation of drugs. Although the Arizona data do not permit a detailed (quantitative) analysis of the amount of drugs possessed at the time of arrest, a review of case records revealed that drug quantities were large and that marijuana was involved in less than 12 percent of the cases. These findings present and identify a population imprisoned for far more severe drug offenses than the population depicted in prior studies.

Although the proportion of marijuana offenders in Arizona is relatively small, marijuana cases were characterized by offenders' extensive and severe criminal history records. Findings on marijuana arrestees showed that they averaged approximately 10 prior arrests and 17 prior offenses (refer to Table 3.19). Also, few of Arizona's marijuana offenders had increases in charges and case severity from arrest to sentencing. In fact, multivariate analysis showed that marijuana offenders were less likely than paraphernalia and dangerous drug offenders to experience case adjustments. Taken together, these findings serve as evidence that marijuana offenders are not first- or second-time offenders and are not treated more harshly or more leniently than other drug offenders.

The bivariate analysis of pre–Proposition 200 data shows that race and ethnicity played a role in charging decisions, with whites having more case adjustments than blacks or Latinos. However, once multivariate analyses were conducted and all controls were included in the analyses, the race effects disappeared. In other words, there were no racial/ethnic disparities in plea outcomes before Proposition 200. Gender, employment status, and legal criteria (e.g., drug sales, paraphernalia cases, dangerous drugs, and prior record) were the significant predictors of plea outcomes.

Findings also show that the majority of low-level drug offenders were probationers. Further, the plea-bargaining processes for arrestees and probationers are clearly different. Probationers were less likely than arrestees to engage in plea-bargaining, and, unlike arrestees, probationers with extensive criminal histories were more likely to see their case sum severity score increase rather than decrease.

Overall, the pre–Proposition 200 findings from this study would seem to lend some support to prosecutors' contentions that low-level offenders in Arizona have more serious and more extensive criminal histories than the "low-level" label suggests. Also, low-level offenders were arrested with relatively large quantities of drugs and allowed to plead down to low-level offenses, distorting the true nature of low-level drug offenders in prison. This also holds true for marijuana offenders whose incarceration appears to be a function of the extent of their criminal record and/or the quantity of drugs they possessed at arrest.

CHAPTER FOUR

Did Prosecution Patterns Resulting in Prison Sentences Change After Ballot Reforms? Findings from Arizona

Introduction

New drug policies continue to be proposed in Arizona as a means to highlight the processing of marijuana cases or as modifications to Proposition 200. On the one hand, proponents of Proposition 200 have been unsuccessful in their attempts to pass a law that would require a state agency to distribute marijuana for medical use as well as their attempts to propose that marijuana possession be subject only to fines.[1] On the other hand, county and state officials have been successful in implementing a law that allows jail time for drug offenders if such offenders commit another drug-related offense, violate their terms of probation, or refuse probation (i.e., drug treatment) altogether.

Given the direct language of Proposition 200 regarding eligibility (i.e., it excludes offenders with a violent offense in their criminal history), we examine whether offenders' records became more serious and lengthy after implementation of the proposition. We also examine the overall prevalence of plea-bargaining to assess if offenders are

---

[1] For example, an initiative on the November 2002 ballot proposed that (1) marijuana be distributed for medical use by the Department of Public Safety; (2) a person could possess marijuana for medial use without a doctor's written prescription; and (3) marijuana possession (two ounces or less) be subject to fines rather than incarceration. This proposition was defeated, however.

now less willing to accept a plea for disposition their cases. It is possible that plea-bargaining may be less prevalent in possession cases where offenders have extensive records. In these cases, offenders no longer see treatment as an incentive to plea-bargain and prosecutors cannot recommend treatment to motivate them to plead down. Lastly, we examine whether sale and paraphernalia charges have a direct influence on plea outcomes after proposition 200. Specifically, we examine if sale charges increased and produced more severe plea outcomes. Also, we test whether paraphernalia charges increased after proposition 200 as a new mechanism to encourage plea-bargaining opportunities.

Population Description

Post–Proposition 200, the overwhelming majority of imprisoned offenders were still male, although the percentage of female arrestees increased after Proposition 200 (12 percent versus 15 percent—refer to Table 3.14). There was a reduction in the percentage of Latino arrestees (36 percent versus 30 percent) while an increase in black arrestees (18 percent versus 22 percent) after the implementation of the proposition. County variation across implementation periods was found in three of the four counties. Specifically, Pima County experienced an increase in the number of probationers incarcerated for low-level drug offenses after Proposition 200, whereas all other counties showed a decline in incarceration of probationers. Sixty percent of the prisoners were on probation prior to imprisonment. The proportion of marijuana arrestees and probationers dropped after Proposition 200. The proportion of dangerous drug and narcotic drug cases also decreased, while paraphernalia cases increased after implementation (26 percent versus 38 percent). A total of 17 percent of arrestees had at least one charge at arrest that involved the sale, transportation, or importation of drugs. The majority of cases were prosecuted through a guilty plea, with fewer than 4 percent of all cases convicted by juries or a judge. After implementation, probations' criminal history records were more extensive in nature. There is relatively minimal change between changes in number and sum severity score from prosecution to sentencing, indicating, as in the pre–Proposition 200 period, that the bargaining process occurs before prosecution. As with probationers, the criminal records of arrestees after implementation appear lengthier. Also, the number of charges and the sum severity score at prosecution changed minimally at the time of sentencing. Arrestees were sentenced to an average of 2.2 years pre–Proposition 200 and 1.9 years after implementation of the law.

The Prosecution of Possessors
To examine whether plea-bargaining practices changed after Proposition 200, we conducted several analyses. Analyses included the examination of how gender and particular drug offenses influenced case adjustments after the implementation of the proposition. Given that the findings show charging processes from arrest to prosecution vary by drug offense and not gender, we restrict our findings in this section to male arrestees (Table 4.1).[2] Among male marijuana arrestees, there were no cases whose charges increased after Proposition 200. Also, the percentage of marijuana cases in which charges decreased increased after Proposition 200. The same pattern exists for dangerous drug, narcotic drug, and vapor-related cases. Narcotic drug offenders had more case adjustments post-Proposition 200 than before the implementation of the law. The percentage of paraphernalia cases with a reduction in charges decreased after Proposition 200 (36 percent versus 25 percent).

The Role of Criminal History
An examination of the relationship between prior record and plea-bargaining (based on change in sum severity score) before and after Proposition 200 shows that arrestees with more extensive and severe prior records were more likely to see a drop in sum severity score before Proposition 200 (see Table 4.2). The only exception to this pattern concerns the effect of mean prior arrests on the no-change outcome. The post-implementation pattern is somewhat different from

---

[2] Male arrestees were selected instead of female arrestees because of the small (at times "0") sample size of females in particular plea outcomes.

Table 4.1

Relationship Among Drug Offense and Offense Charges—Male
Arrestees Only

	Pre–Proposition 200 Average (%)	Post–Proposition 200 Average (%)
Marijuana		
Charges increased	7.4	0.0
No change	70.7	71.9
Charges decreased	21.9	28.1
Dangerous drugs		
Charges increased	4.3	13.0
No change	0.2	54.8
Charges decreased	5.4	32.0
Narcotic drugs		
Charges increased	4.9	15.4
No change	72.2	54.1
Charges decreased	22.9	30.5
Paraphernalia		
Charges increased	12.7	6.8
No change	50.9	68.4
Charges decreased	36.4	24.9
Vapor-related substances		
Charges increased	0.0	0.0
No change	77.9	75.0
Charges decreased	22.1	25.0

NOTE: Analysis includes change in charges from arrest to prosecution.

the pre-implementation period. Post-implementation analyses show
that the lengthier and more severe the prior record, the more likely
prisoners were to have their sum severity score increase from arrest to
prosecution. Also, offenders with less extensive records were more
likely to see no change in sum severity score. In sum, post-
proposition data show that prior record was more extensive and severe in nature and less varied across the severity score outcomes.

Table 4.2
Relationship Between Criminal History Record and Sum Severity Score—
Arrestees Only

	Pre–Proposition 200		Post–Proposition 200	
	Average	SD	Average	SD
Arrest to prosecution: offense severity increased				
Mean number of prior arrests***	7.5	6.2	13.9	15.1
Mean number of prior offenses	19.7	15.4	26.5	18.4
Mean severity score—prior offenses	729.0	570.1	1,082.8	808.8
Arrest to prosecution: no change				
Mean number of prior arrests***	10.0	8.5	12.2	12.2
Mean number of prior offenses	20.0	16.5	24.4	21.5
Mean severity score—prior offenses	806.9	633.4	1,008.0	927.6
Arrest to prosecution: offense severity decreased				
Mean number of prior arrests***	9.6	8.4	12.8	8.4
Mean number of prior offenses	20.1	14.9	25.7	14.4
Mean severity score—prior offenses	816.1	614.2	1,013.3	581.4

NOTE: Statistical differences of variables across time periods are presented here.
*** $p < .001$.

The Role of Race

Although several patterns emerged based on the role of race and plea-bargaining post–Proposition 200, these findings should be interpreted with caution given the relative small number of cases in particular charging outcomes (see Table 4.3). First, there were no black offenders whose charges increased in number from arrest to prosecution in any drug offense. Second, charges were increased for Latinos convicted of dangerous drug, narcotic drug, and paraphernalia cases in a higher percentage of cases than for whites and blacks. Third, blacks and Latinos had fewer case adjustments than whites in paraphernalia cases.

Table 4.3
Relationship Among Drug Offense, Race/Ethnicity, and Offense Charges—Arrestees Only

	Marijuana, (%)	Dangerous Drugs, (%)	Narcotic Drugs, (%)	Paraphernalia, (%)
Whites				
Charges increased	0.0	11.4	6.1	10.3
No change	100.0	55.3	72.7	47.4
Charges decreased	0.0	33.3	21.2	42.3
Blacks				
Charges increased	0.0	0.0	0.0	0.0
No change	62.5	25.0	48.9	95.5
Charges decreased	37.5	75.0	51.1	4.5
Latinos				
Charges increased	6.5	20.0	30.4	15.7
No change	61.3	40.0	54.9	80.4
Charges decreased	32.2	40.0	14.7	3.9

NOTES: Analyses include change in charges from arrest to prosecution. Vapor-related offenses and cases involving Native Americans and other racial/ethnic groups are not presented here because of their small representation in the overall population of cases.

Case Severity in Plea-Bargaining

Because the number of blacks, marijuana cases, and cases from Yuma and Mohave Counties with case severity increases post-Proposition 200 were so few in number (in some cases, "0" was in the cells), they have been excluded from the multivariate analyses.[3] Latino offenders were more likely than white offenders to have an increase in sum severity score (see Table 4.4). Offenders who were employed were less likely than unemployed offenders to have an increase in sum severity score. Also, dangerous drug cases were less likely than paraphernalia cases to have charges decrease. Cases with a drug sale charge at arrest

---

[3] To determine the effect of blacks, marijuana cases, and Yuma and Mohave counties on plea outcomes, we conducted a logistic regression analysis (a decrease in severity was coded "1" and no change was coded "0"). Findings from this analysis show that age, being a Latino, and being sentenced in Pima County had a negative effect on plea-bargaining, while number of counts had a positive effect on this binary measure. No other variables were significant predictors, indicating no lost effects from the utilization of a multinomial model to predict change in sum severity score.

Table 4.4
Multinomial Estimates of Charge(s), Sum Severity Score—
Post–Proposition 200

	Increase in Severity		Decrease in Severity	
	ß (SE)	Exp (ß)	ß (SE)	Exp (ß)
Intercept[a]	−0.338 (1.139)		−8.632 (1.706)	
Male	0.23 (0.425)	1.269	−0.299 (0.394)	0.742
Latino	0.997*** (0.380)	2.71	−0.528 (0.334)	0.589
Age at sentencing	0.005 (0.021)	1.005	−0.024 (0.018)	0.976
Employment	−0.995* (0.415)	0.369	0.054 (0.314)	1.055
Dangerous drugs	−0.141 (0.458)	0.868	−1.089** (0.373)	0.337
Narcotic drugs	−0.600 (0.432)	0.549	-0.382 (0.376)	0.682
Drug sale charge	0.720 (0.396)	2.054	0.984** (0.340)	2.675
Counts at arrest	0.202 (0.213)	1.223	1.609*** (0.207)	4.997
Prior offenses in record	0.002 (0.008)	1.002	0.002 (0.010)	1.002
Pima County	1.422*** (0.358)	4.145	−4.298*** (1.118)	0.014
Mohave County	0.666 (0.534)	1.946	−0.774 (0.525)	0.461

−2 Log Likelihood = 630.9
Chi-Square = 253.03; df = 22

NOTE: Analysis includes only arrestees.
[a] Reference category includes No change in sum severity score, Whites, Paraphernalia cases, and Maricopa County.
* $p < 0.05$; ** $p < 0.01$; *** $p < 0.001$.

were more likely to have a decrease in severity score. A higher number of counts at arrest increased the likelihood of a reduction in severity score. Offenders convicted in Pima County were more likely to have an increase in severity score and less likely to have a decrease than offenders convicted in Maricopa County.

Summary and Policy Implications for Arizona Pre– and Post–Proposition 200

The post–Proposition 200 findings from Arizona show changes in prosecution and sentencing-related patterns. After Proposition 200, incarcerated offenders had more extensive and severe criminal records, which may be attributed to the fact that those offenders were ineligible for treatment and the possibility of increased rates of probation revocations for offenders with more extensive records. Evidence of post–Proposition 200 "hardening" in the processing of low-level drug offenders is reflected in the finding that the proportion of prosecuted and imprisoned drug cases involving paraphernalia cases increased after Proposition 200. The uncertainty regarding how paraphernalia cases should be processed (at least until Arizona's Supreme Court decided the issue) may be the reason for such an increase. Some jurisdictions treated paraphernalia cases as eligible for treatment under the new law, while others excluded them altogether. Also, the proportion of paraphernalia cases in which charges were reduced decreased after Proposition 200, revealing a tightening in bargaining practices among cases not specifically outlined in the original proposition.

Additionally, arrestees with more extensive criminal histories were more likely to have the severity of charges increase in severity after Proposition 200. The net effect of this change is more punitive treatment because prior record may now serve to enhance rather than to reduce punishment, which was the case prior to the implementation of the proposition. Interestingly, the proportion of marijuana offenders not only decreased after implementation but those offenders were also far less likely to have an increase in severity score from arrest to sentencing. Post-proposition prosecutorial decisionmaking processes appear to be characterized by decreased severity for marijuana cases, increased severity for paraphernalia cases, and increased severity for cases with extensive prior records.

One additional post–Proposition 200 change involved the role of race in plea outcomes. In contrast to the pre–Proposition 200 findings, no black prisoners were treated more severely after the implementation of Proposition 200. However, post–Proposition 200 data indicate that Latinos were treated more severely than other racial/ethnic groups. These findings should be interpreted with caution given the relatively small number of cases in specific charging outcomes.

The findings from the Arizona component of the study demonstrate the extensive use of plea-bargaining in the prosecution of imprisoned low-level drug offenders, with the vast majority of case charge and/or severity adjustments being made between the arrest and prosecution stages and comparatively few adjustments being made between prosecution and sentencing. The overwhelming majority of cases (96–97 percent) involved guilty pleas. These analyses show the more complex nature of guilty pleas (i.e., no change in case severity, a decrease in case severity, and an increase in case severity from arrest to sentencing) and how case status (probationer versus arrestee) and legal criteria differentially influence plea outcomes.

CHAPTER FIVE

Lessons from California and Arizona Drug Sentencing Reforms

In conducting this study, we set out to fill in gaps in our knowledge about the prosecution of imprisoned low-level drug offenders and how it is affected by diversion-based drug reforms. Specifically, we wanted to generate more basic information on the characteristics of imprisoned low-level drug offenders. In essence, the study was designed to assess what proportion of those sentenced to prison on low-level drug charges had merely "smoked a joint" (that is, the true underlying drug crime was minor) and had no or minimal prior record (that is, they were first-time offenders) versus the proportion that had pled down from a more severe crime or had a severe criminal record. Answering these questions is important because the ballot initiatives were generally intended to divert the former category of offender from the prison track, and it is from these diversions that the anticipated savings were expected.

Within the category of low-level drug offenders, we examined marijuana offenders to determine whether they were being prosecuted "too harshly" relative to the prosecution of other drugs. Given the extensive body of research on racial disparities in the criminal justice process, we also examined the role of race and ethnicity in plea-bargaining and sentencing of low-level drug offenders. Another focus of the study was a more general examination of the role of plea-bargaining in drug prosecutions and those factors affecting plea-bargaining. Finally, the passage of Proposition 200 in Arizona in

1996 afforded the opportunity to examine the effect of that reform on drug prosecution and imprisonment.

In sum, from a policy perspective, plea-bargaining, a widely accepted practice, appears to be used not only in the prosecution of drug offenses that result in prison sentences but also in a manner consistent with prosecutorial practices aimed at incarcerating drug offenders who are perceived to present a greater threat to the community due to more extensive criminal involvement, involvement in more serious forms of drug offenses, or both. The prosecution, sentencing, and incarceration of low-level drug offenses, while complex, does not appear to be a practice that is particularly harsh in that low-level drug offenders who go to prison are often much more than low-level offenders. In fact, they tend to have criminal histories that reflect their involvement in a variety of criminal offenses.

Prosecution patterns changed after the implementation of Proposition 200, with a marked increase in the prosecution and incarceration of paraphernalia offenders. Although some have argued that this shift is a way to circumvent the intent of the proposition, incarcerated paraphernalia offenders share many of the characteristics of other low-level drug offenders—they have extensive criminal offense histories. In sum, it does not appear that new prosecution practices evolved after Proposition 200 that had the effect of blocking the diversion to treatment of drug offenders and resulted in the incarceration of scores of nonserious offenders.

The finding that Latinos have been dealt with more severely after Proposition 200 is troubling, although this finding must be interpreted with great caution because of the number of Latino offenders examined in these analyses. However, further examination of this finding is necessary. Additionally, given that the pathway to incarceration for the majority of Arizona's low-level drug offenders is probation, there is a need for additional research that examines the decisionmaking practices that lead to probation revocation and incarceration. Research will need to go beyond the prosecution function and examine the role of probation officials in making those decisions as well as the decisionmaking processes that lead to the chain of events culminating in the incarceration of low-level drug offenders.

Classification of California and Arizona Drug Offenses

Tables A.1 and A.2 show whether we counted an offense as low level. In California and Arizona, we counted offenses to which Propositions 36 or 200 fully or partially applied as low level. We also list nonqualifying (or non–low level) offenses so that the reader has a better understanding of sales, trafficking, and other offenses that are used as points of comparison throughout the book.

Table A.1
California Drug Offenses and Their Eligibility Under Proposition 36

Prop 36 Application	Code Provision	Department of Corrections Coding	Short Description
		Possession	
NA	H&S11350	CS+Possession	See below
Yes	H&S11350(a)	CS+Possession	Possession of designated controlled substances
Yes	H&S11350(b)	CS+Possession	Possession of designated controlled substances
Arguably	H&S11370.1(a)	CS+Possession	Possession of certain controlled substances while armed with a firearm
Yes	H&S11377	CS+Possession	Unauthorized possession
Yes	H&S11377(a)	CS+Possession	See above
NA	H&S11500	CS+Possession	Prosecution by district attorney, attorney general, or special counsel

Table A.1—continued

Prop 36 Application	Code Provision	Department of Corrections Coding	Short Description
No	P4573.8	CS+Possession	Unauthorized possession of drugs or alcoholic beverages in prison, camp, jail, etc.
Possession for Sale			
No	H&S11351	CS+Possession for sale, etc.	Possession or purchase for sale of designated controlled substances
No	H&S11351.5	CS+Possession for sale, etc.	Possession of cocaine base for sale
No	H&S11375	CS+Possession for sale, etc.	Possession for sale or sale of designated controlled substances
No	H&S11378	CS+Possession for sale, etc.	Possession for sale
No	H&S11378.5	CS+Possession for sale, etc.	Possession for sale of designated substances including phencyclidine
NA	H&S11379	CS+Possession for sale, etc.	See below
In part	H&S11379(a)	CS+Possession for sale, etc.	Transportation, sale, furnishing, etc.
No	H&S11379(b)	CS+Possession for sale, etc.	Transportation, sale, furnishing, etc.
No	H&S11379.2	CS+Possession for sale, etc.	Possession for sale or sale of ketamine
NA	H&S11379.5	CS+Possession for sale, etc.	See below
In part	H&S11379.5(a)	CS+Possession for sale, etc.	Transportation, sale, furnishing, etc. of designated substances including phencyclidine
No	H&S11379.5(b)	CS+Possession for sale, etc.	Transportation, sale, furnishing, etc. of designated substances including phencyclidine
NA	H&S11500.5 (repealed— shift to 11351)	CS+Possession for sale, etc.	N/A

Table A.1—continued

Prop 36 Application	Code Provision	Department of Corrections Coding	Short Description
		Sales	
NA	H&S11352	CS+Sales, etc.	See below
In part	H&S11352(a)	CS+Sales, etc.	Transportation, sale, giving away, etc. of designated controlled substances
No	H&S11352(b)	CS+Sales, etc.	Transportation, etc. of controlled substances
No	H&S11353.7	CS+Sales, etc.	Adult sale or gift of controlled substance to minor in public parks
No	P4573.9	CS+Sales, etc.	Selling etc. by person not in custody to person in custody, in prison etc.
		Manufacturing	
No	H&S11104	CS+Manufacturing	Furnishing substances etc. for manufacturing purposes
No	H&S11366.6	CS+Manufacturing	Utilizing building, room, space, or enclosure designed to suppress law enforcement entry in order to sell, manufacture, or possess for sale specified controlled substances
No	H&S11379.6(a)	CS+Manufacturing	Manufacturing, compounding, converting, producing, etc.
No	H&S11379.6(b)	CS+Manufacturing	Manufacturing, compounding, converting, producing, etc.
NA	H&S11383	CS+Manufacturing	See below
No	H&S11383(a)	CS+Manufacturing	Possession with intent to manufacture
No	H&S11383(b)	CS+Manufacturing	Possession with intent to manufacture
NA	H&S11383(c)	CS+Manufacturing	See below
No	H&S11383(c)(1)	CS+Manufacturing	Possession with intent to manufacture
No	H&S11383(c)(2)	CS+Manufacturing	Possession with intent to manufacture
No	B&P4324(a)	CS+Other	Forged prescriptions; possession by forged prescription

Table A.1—continued

Prop 36 Application	Code Provision	Department of Corrections Coding	Short Description
Arguably	B&P4324(b)	CS+Other	Forged prescriptions; possession by forged prescription
No	H&S11154	CS+Other	Prescription, administration or furnishing controlled substances, restrictions
No	H&S11173	CS+Other	Fraud, deceit, misrepresentations
No	H&S11353	CS+Other	Adult inducing minor to violate provisions; use or employment of minors
No	H&S11353.5	CS+Other	Controlled substances given away or sold to minors; locations where children are present
No	H&S11355	CS+Other	Sale or furnishing substance falsely represented to be a controlled substance
No	H&S11364.7(b)	CS+Other	Delivering, furnishing, transferring, possessing, or manufacture with intent to deliver, furnish, transfer, or manufacture drug paraphernalia
No	H&S11366	CS+Other	Opening or maintenance of unlawful places
No	H&S11366.5(a)	CS+Other	Renting, leasing, or making available for use a building, room, space, or enclosure for unlawful manufacture, storage, or distribution of controlled substance; allowing building, room, space, or enclosure to be fortified to suppress law enforcement entry to further sale of specified controlled substances

Table A.1—continued

Prop 36 Application	Code Provision	Department of Corrections Coding	Short Description
Arguably	H&S11366.8(a)	CS+Other	Construction, possession, or use of false compartment with intent to conceal controlled substance punished by imprisonment in a county jail for a term of imprisonment not to exceed one year or in the state prison
Arguably	H&S11366.8(b)	CS+Other	Construction, possession, or use of false compartment with intent to conceal controlled substance
Arguably	H&S11368	CS+Other	Forged or altered prescriptions
No	H&S11370.6	CS+Other	Possession of moneys or negotiable instruments in excess of $100,000 involved in unlawful sale or purchase of any controlled substance
No	H&S11370.9	CS+Other	Proceeds over $25,000 derived from controlled substance offenses
No	H&S11371	CS+Other	Prescription violations; inducing minor to violate provisions
No	H&S11374.5	CS+Other	Manufacturer violating hazardous substance disposal law by disposal of controlled substance or its precursor requests the prosecuting authority to seek recovery of that cost
No	H&S11380	CS+Other	Adult using minor as agent; inducing or furnishing to minor
No	H&S11382	CS+Other	Sale or furnishing substances falsely represented to be a controlled substance
NA	H&S11501	CS+Other	Action to recover funds expended in investigation of violations of controlled substances regulations

Table A.1—continued

Prop 36 Application	Code Provision	Department of Corrections Coding	Short Description
Arguably	H&S11550(e)	CS+Other	Unlawful acts; rehabilitation programs; possession of firearms; diversion punishable by imprisonment in county jail for not exceeding one year or in state prison
Arguably	H&S11550(f)	CS+Other	Unlawful acts; penalties; rehabilitation programs; possession of firearms; diversion
Arguably/ in part	P4573	CS+Other	Controlled substances; bringing into prison, etc.
No	P4573.6	CS+Other	Unauthorized possession of CS in prison, etc.
No	P653F(d)	CS+Other	Soliciting commission of certain offenses
Arguably/ in part	W&I1001.5	CS+Other	Bringing or sending contraband into grounds of or possession in Youth Authority institutions
Yes	H&S11357	Hashish Possession	Unauthorized possession
No	H&S11359	Marijuana Possession for Sale	Possession for sale
In part	H&S11360	Marijuana Sales	Transportation, sale, import, give away, etc.
NA	H&S11360(a)	Marijuana Sales	See above
No	H&S11358	Other Marijuana Offenses	Unauthorized cultivation, harvesting or processing
No	H&S11361(a)	Other Marijuana Offenses	Adults employing or selling to minors; minors under or over 14 years of age
No	H&S11361(b)	Other Marijuana Offenses	Adults employing or selling to minors; minors under or over 14 years of age
No	V23152	Driving Under the Influence	Driving under influence; blood alcohol percentage
No	V23152(a)	Driving Under the Influence	See above
No	V23152(b)	Driving Under the Influence	See above

Table A.1—continued

Prop 36 Application	Code Provision	Department of Corrections Coding	Short Description
No	V23153	Driving Under the Influence	Driving under the influence and causing bodily injury to another person; blood alcohol percentage
No	V23153(a)	Driving Under the Influence	See above
No	V23153(b)	Driving Under the Influence	See above
No	V23190	Driving Under the Influence	Repeated conviction of violation of §23153; great bodily injury

NOTES: CS = Controlled substance; NA = not applicable.

Table A.2
Arizona Drug Offenses and Their Eligibility Under Proposition 200

Prop 200 Application	Code Provision	Short Description
In part	13-3402	Possession and sale of peyote; classification
In part	13-3403	Possession and sale of a vapor-releasing substance containing a toxic substance; regulation of sale; exceptions; classification
No	13-3404	Sale of precursor chemicals; report; exemptions; violation; classification
In part, if precursor chemical is included in Schedules I–V	13-3404.01	Possession of precursor chemicals II; classification
Yes	13-3405(B)(1)	Possession, use, production, sale, or transportation of marijuana; classification
Yes	13-3405(B)(2)	Possession, use, production, sale, or transportation of marijuana; classification
Yes	13-3405(B)(3)	Possession, use, production, sale, or transportation of marijuana; classification
In part	13-3405(B)(10)	Possession, use, production, sale, or transportation of marijuana; classification
In part	13-3405(B)(11)	Possession, use, production, sale, or transportation of marijuana; classification

Table A.2—continued

Prop 200 Application	Code Provision	Short Description
Yes	13-3407(B)(1)	Possession, use, administration, acquisition, sale, manufacture, or transportation of dangerous drugs; classification
In part	13-3407(B)(7)	Possession, use, administration, acquisition, sale, manufacture, or transportation of dangerous drugs; classification
Yes	13-3408(B)(1)	Possession, use, administration, acquisition, sale, manufacture, or transportation of narcotic drugs; classification
In part	13-3408(B)(7)	Possession, use, administration, acquisition, sale, manufacture or transportation of narcotic drugs; classification
In part	13-3415(A)	Possession, manufacture, delivery and advertisement of drug paraphernalia; definitions; violation; classification; civil forfeiture; factors

Cases Relevant to Study

State v. Estrada, 34 P.3d 356 (Ariz. 2001): "The probation eligibility provisions of Proposition 200 apply to convictions for the possession of items of drug paraphernalia associated solely with personal use by individuals also charged or who could have been charged with simple use or possession of a controlled substance under the statute. The concurring opinion urges the court to extend the application of Proposition 200 to include persons found exclusively in possession of paraphernalia but without the presence of illegal drugs: Court states: "This argument raises the separate question whether the probation eligibility provisions can be applied to a 'stand-alone' paraphernalia charge. We decline to address the question for two reasons. First, the stand-alone case is not presented on this record. . . . Second, and more importantly, Proposition 200, by its own terms, depends on the actual presence of drugs. Accordingly, we have no authority to expand the Proposition to cover circumstances in which drugs are not present. Further extension is necessarily a matter for the legislature." Resolves conflict between two courts of appeal. Previously, in *State v. Holm*, 985 P.2d 527 (App.1998), Division Two concluded that drug paraphernalia charges fell outside of Prop. 200, while the instant cases came from Division One, which concluded that drug paraphernalia charges fell within scope of Prop. 200. Supreme Court reasoned that the legislature did not intend to incarcerate for the lesser offense and mandate probation for the more serious offense.

Table A.2—continued

Cases Relevant to Study

State v. Roman, 30 P.3d 661 (App.2002): Promoting prison contraband does not fall within Prop. 200. "[S]ection 13-2505 does not simply proscribe the personal possession or use of drugs; it proscribes 'promoting prison contraband.' Moreover, Section 13-901.01 does not include promoting contraband within one of the offenses mandating probation, nor do the purposes of Proposition 200 indicate that it was intended to apply to such an offense. The legislature chose long ago to treat the possession of a controlled substance in a correctional facility more severely than mere possession."

State v. Pereyra, 18 P.3d 146 (App. 2001): Personal possession of a controlled substance in a drug-free school zone falls within Prop. 200 (Section 13-901.01).

State v. Ossana, 18 P.3d 1258 (App. 2001): "[F]or a defendant to be excluded from the mandatory probation of Section 13-901.01(A), the prior convictions must be for possession or use, not merely for attempted possession or use."

State v. Guillory, 18 P.3d 1261 (Ariz. App. 2001): Drug-related crimes "equally as serious as the specifically enumerated crimes in subsection (G) of personal possession or use of a controlled substance" are included within the meaning of Section 13-901.01.

Stubblefield v. Trombino, 4 P.3d 437 (Ariz. App. 2000): Proposition 200 was enacted to ensure drug treatment and drug education for offenders. It would, therefore, "be illogical to hold that Proposition 200 applies to possession of narcotic drugs but that it does not apply to the less serious offense of attempted possession of narcotic drugs."

In re. Fernando, 986 P.2d 901 (App.1999): Prop. 200 does not apply to juveniles.

NOTES: Prop. 200 did not include "transfer for personal use." It is thus not clear whether an individual may be charged with "transferring" in order to avoid the Prop. 200 charge of "possession."

References

Albonetti, Celesta A. 1997. "Sentencing under the Federal Sentencing Guidelines: Effects of Defendant Characteristics, Guilty Pleas, and Departures on Sentence Outcomes for Drug Offenses, 1991–1992." *Law & Society Review* 31(4), 34.

Austin, James, John Clark, Patricia Hardyman, and D. Alan Henry. 1999. "The Impact of 'Three Strikes and You're Out.'" *Punishment & Society* 1(2), 32.

Berlin, E. P. 1993. "Federal Sentencing Guidelines' Failure to Eliminate Sentencing Disparity: Governmental Manipulations Before Arrest." *Wisconsin Law Review* 1993(1), 187–230.

Bernstein, F. A. 1995. "Discretion Redux: Mandatory Minimums, Federal Judges, and the 'Safety Valve' Provision of the 1994 Crime Act." *University of Dayton Law Review* 20(2), 765–778.

Bureau of Justice Statistics (BJS). 2000. *Prisoners in 1999.* Washington, D.C.: U.S. Department of Justice.

Caulkins, Jonathan P., C. Peter Rydell, William Schwabe, and James R. Chiesa. 1997. *Mandatory Minimum Drug Sentences: Throwing Away the Key or the Taxpayers' Money?* Santa Monica, Calif.: RAND Corporation, MR-827-DPRC.

Forst, Brian. 1995. "Prosecution and Sentencing." In *Crime.* Eds. J. Q. Wilson and J. Petersilia. San Francisco: Institute for Contemporary Studies.

Greenwood, Peter W., Karyn E. Model, C. Peter Rydell, and James R. Chiesa. 1998. *Diverting Children from a Life of Crime: Measuring Costs and Benefits.* Santa Monica, Calif.: RAND Corporation, MR-699-1-UCB/RC/IF.

Hagan, John. 1981. "Sentence Bargaining in Federal District Courts." In *Plea-Bargaining,* Eds. W. McDonald and J. Cramer. Lexington, Mass: Lexington Press.

Human Rights Watch. 1997. *Cruel and Unusual: Disproportionate Sentences for New York Drug Offenders.* New York: Human Rights Watch.

Karoly, Lynn A., Peter W. Greenwood, Susan S. Everingham, Jill Hoube, M. Rebecca Kilburn, C. Peter Rydell, Matthew R. Sanders, and James R. Chiesa. 1998. *Investing in Our Children: What We Know and Don't Know About the Costs and Benefits of Early Childhood Interventions.* Santa Monica, Calif.: RAND Corporation, MR-898-TCWF.

Kautt, P., and C. Spohn. 2002. "Crack-Ing Down on Black Drug Offenders? Testing for Interactions Among Offenders' Race, Drug Type, and Sentencing Strategy in Federal Drug Sentences." *Justice Quarterly: JQ* 19, Part 1, 1–36.

Males, Mike, Daniel Macallair, Cheryl Rios, and Deborah Vargas. 2000. *Drug Use and Justice: An Examination of California Drug Policy Enforcement.* Washington, D.C.: Justice Policy Institute.

Miethe, Terance D. 1987. "Charging and Plea-Bargaining Practices Under Determinate Sentencing: An Investigation of the Hydraulic Displacement of Discretion." *The Journal of Criminal Law and Criminology* 78(1), 155–176.

Moore, C. A., and T. D. Miethe. 1986. "Regulated and Unregulated Sentencing Decisions—An Analysis of First-Year Practices Under Minnesota's Felony Sentencing Guidelines." *Law and Society Review* 20(2), 253–277.

Nagel, I. H. 1990. "Structuring Sentencing Discretion: The New Federal Sentencing Guidelines." *Journal of Criminal Law and Criminology* 80(4), 883-943.

Norris, Mikki, Chris Conrad, and Virginia Resner. 1998. *Shattered Lives: Portraits from America's Drug War.* El Cerrito, Calif.: Creative Xpressions.

Orloff, Thomas. 2000. *Getting the Facts About Proposition 36.* Sacramento: California District Attorneys' Association.

Reitz, Kevin R. 1993. "Sentencing Reform in the States: An Overview of the Colorado Law Review Symposium." *University of Colorado Law Review* 64(3), 645.

Rhodes, W. 1991. "Federal Criminal Sentencing: Some Measurement Issues with Application to Pre-Guideline Sentencing Disparity." *Journal of Criminal Law and Criminology* 81(4), 1002–1033.

Riley, K. Jack, Patricia A. Ebener, James Chiesa, Susan Turner, and Jeanne Ringel. 2000. *Drug Offenders and the Criminal Justice System: Will Proposition 3 Treat or Create Problems?* Santa Monica, Calif.: RAND Corporation, IP-204.

Roberts, Julian V. 1994. "The Role of Criminal Record in the Federal Sentencing Guidelines." *Criminal Justice Ethics* 13(1), 21.

Schulhofer, S. J. 1992. "Assessing the Federal Sentencing Process: The Problem Is Uniformity, Not Disparity." *American Criminal Law Review* 29(3), 833–873.

Sentencing Project. 1998. *Drug Policy and the Criminal Justice System.* Washington D.C.: The Sentencing Project, 1998.

Sevigny, E. L., and J. P. Caulkins. 2004. "Kingpins or Mules: An Analysis of Drug Offenders Incarcerated in Federal and State Prisons." *Criminology and Public Policy,* 3(3), July, 401–434.

Speiglman, Richard, Dorie Klein, Robin Miller, and Amanda Noble. 2003. "Early Implementation of Proposition 36: Criminal Justice and Treatment System Issues in Eight Counties." *Journal of Psychoactive Drugs* 35 Suppl 1: 133–141.

Standen, Jeffrey. 1993. "Plea-Bargaining in the Shadow of the Guidelines." *California Law Review* 81(6), 1471.

Tonry, Michael H. 1996. *Sentencing Matters: Studies in Crime and Public Policy.* New York: Oxford University Press.

Tonry, Michael, and John C. Coffee Jr. 1992. "Plea-Bargaining and Enforcement of Sentencing Guidelines." In *Principled Sentencing.* Eds. A. V. Hirsch and A. Ashworth. Boston: Northeastern University Press, 308–324.

Ulmer, Jeffery T., and John H. Kramer. 1996. "Court Communities Under Sentencing Guidelines: Dilemmas of Formal Rationality and Sentencing Disparity." *Criminology* 34(3), 26.

United States Sentencing Commission. 1995. *Cocaine and Federal Sentencing Policy.* Washington, D.C.

Vera Institute of Justice. 1977. *Felony Arrests, Their Prosecution and Disposition in New York City's Courts.* A Vera Institute of Justice monograph. New York: Vera Institute of Justice.

Yellen, David. 1993. "Illusion, Illogic, and Injustice: Real-Offense Sentencing and the Federal Sentencing Guidelines." *Minnesota Law Review* 78(2), 403.

Zatz, M. S. 1984. "Race, Ethnicity, and Determinate Sentencing—A New Dimension to an Old Controversy." *Criminology* 22(2), 147–171.